ADAPTIVE RIFLE
For Performance Shooting

BEN STOEGER & JOEL PARK

Skyhorse Publishing

Skyhorse Publishing books may be purchased in bulk at special discounts for sales promotion, corporate gifts, fund-raising, or educational purposes. Special editions can also be created to specifications. For details, contact the Special Sales Department, Skyhorse Publishing, 307 West 36th Street, 11th Floor, New York, NY 10018 or info@skyhorsepublishing.com.

Skyhorse® and Skyhorse Publishing® are registered trademarks of Skyhorse Publishing, Inc.®, a Delaware corporation.

Visit our website at www.skyhorsepublishing.com.

Please follow our publisher Tony Lyons on Instagram @tonylyonsisuncertain.

10 9 8 7 6 5 4 3 2 1

Library of Congress Cataloging-in-Publication Data is available on file.

Print ISBN: 978-1-5107-7946-4
eBook ISBN: 978-1-5107-7947-1

Cover design by David Ter-Avanesyan

Printed in China

CONTENTS

DRILLS

ACKNOWLEDGMENTS

Many people helped and supported the creation of this book. There are too many to name them all, but we would like to mention a few who - without their help - this book would not be what it is.

Thank you to:

The group of proofreaders for the ideas, corrections, and additional content they suggested. Special mention to Matt Pranka, Lucas Botkin, Max Latulippe, Josh M., Jon Anderson, Nick Young, and Chris Palmer.

Hwansik Kim for his countless contributions to shooting and training through his very innovative drills and analytical mind.

Jamie Watts for the invaluable help with proofing, editing, formatting and logic checking this book as it went through various phases.

Kenny Nguyen for the training and support for building the corrective diagrams and graphics.

Jenny Cook for her expertise and experience in turning this book into a final product and getting ideas implemented.

From Ben: Tim Meyers hassles me about deadlines and keeps me on task. Countless others helped me in some way. There are too many to mention.

From Joel: My parents for always being encouraging and supportive of my desire to spend all my free time shooting guns in dirt pits. Kenny Nguyen and Jon Anderson for being my tech support and personal gunsmiths as I frequently reconfigure my carbines. Jamie Watts for all the help, perspectives, and encouragement. Many people have influenced my shooting and training over the years. There are too many to name and I am incredibly grateful to all of them.

FOREWORD

Shooting is simple; learning how to train is the hard part. For years I didn't understand this concept. When I got my first AR-15 in 2011, I was shooting chunks of wood on a log with a .22 conversion kit. I slowly progressed through my journey of purchasing equipment, researching different gear on forums, and attending my local IDPA competitions. In 2013 and 2014, I slowly leveled up my training with my growing perspective. I incorporated shot timers, chased the latest trend on the newly formed social media gun culture, looked for shooting standards from the very few instructors on the internet at the time, and even created a few of my own drills for people to try. But I didn't have a solid training plan. I didn't know how to train. I knew how to drive to the range, load mags, set up targets and start blasting, but I also knew I wanted to get better . . . somehow.

What I've described is the training progression for most shooters, whether they're new gun owners or the people who say they grew up with firearms but lack perspective in purposeful training and skill. People only consider training to the level they are familiar with. If they only know shooting soda cans on a log during a 4th of July barbeque, then that will be their standard for being a "marksman" or "really good at shooting."

When I started to research how to train, I found that people generally fell into two camps with their training methodology: train often with professional veterans at two-day courses or shoot competitions regularly. This was concerning to me, since I was already putting most of my time into my rapidly growing company and didn't want to take the time to travel all over the country to get good at shooting. I figured I could learn on my own and would just need to be disciplined about it, but I'd have to figure that part out on my own.

So, I bought my first pallet of ammo (100,000 rounds) at the end of 2017 for around $22,000. Half 9mm, half 5.56. This was my first large expense not directly tied to my business and its operation. I figured spending lots of time and reps would make me a good shooter. I was half right. While reps and time on firearms doesn't hurt, reps are only as useful as how effective your drills, mental focus and personal determination are. I shot another 80,000 rounds the next year, but slowly trimmed it down to 50-60,000 per year as my priorities at work and training methodology changed. While there was growth in shooting all this ammo, it was slow because of my limited knowledge in how to train.

Before investing all this time and money into training, I believed someone could teach themselves how to shoot - with guidance (when possible/needed), perspective from external sources on the internet, purposeful self-analysis, and the discipline to make every rep count. At that time, very few materials existed that could take people from point A to Z in the most efficient way possible. There were some detailed materials out there for people who already possessed a mid-level understanding of shooting, but not much for the new gun owner or noncompetitive shooter.

Enter . . . *Adaptive Rifle*. An ultimate guide, if not the ultimate guide, for learning how to train shooting well, regardless of your current skill level and perspective. Don't be misled into thinking this book only helps you get proficient at shooting rifles or only in a competition setting. The concepts, principles, and decades of experience represented in these pages translate excellently to pistol shooting and other firearm disciplines.

This book would have saved me over $40,000.

I'm focusing on the financial aspect because it's often the first thing people blame when making excuses for not being a good shooter. With that said, the reality is that most people can't afford to shoot weekly, let alone 50,000 rounds a year. In my experience, having had access to excessive amounts of ammo to get good at shooting, it's not necessary to build a high standard of competence. Discipline, perspective, dryfire, and purposeful livefire is how you get good at shooting efficiently even if you can only livefire once a month.

I taught myself how to shoot. You can too. This book will expedite that process.

—Lucas Botkin

Lucas Botkin - @lucastrexarms
https://www.trex-arms.com/

INTRODUCTION

My career shooting rifles, specifically AR-style carbines, began with the military in the early 1990s. I started with what would be considered a very traditional rifle - the M16A2 - doing basic qualification courses with the Marine Corps infantry. One of the things I found very interesting at the time was how much time we spent dryfiring before qualifications. I remember going to fields at Camp Horno while I was stationed at Camp Pendleton, California. We would march out there in full gear with our rifles to find four or five white 55-gallon barrels with small silhouettes painted on them. The silhouettes were painted in different sizes to represent the different distances you would shoot in the qualification; these ranged from 75 to 500 yards. This qualification process was tedious and done with very little instruction - "snapping in," they called it. I didn't know it at the time, but this was my first exposure to what I now know as "dryfire."

My journey with rifles progressed through the years and allowed me to have some interesting experiences. I started by shooting targets that were set out at intermediate distances with my M16A2 (which had a big flashlight strapped to the handguard) and progressed to very basic CQB training with that same setup. At the time, the gear and equipment were very primitive. As I progressed through different units, I switched to a Heckler and Koch MP5N with Surefire handguards. I ultimately ended up with a more modern setup, an M4 Carbine SOPMOD (Special Operations Peculiar MODification kit). That setup was very similar to the rifles I shoot today. The gear evolved and equipment changed as fast as the requirements did. The one consistent factor that never changed was the requirement to be able to shoot your primary weapon - the rifle - accurately and aggressively.

In a peacetime military, nearly every piece of information becomes based in theory. After September 11, 2001, this was no longer an issue. As the Global War on Terrorism progressed, information trickled back from guys on deployments that either supported our ideas about what we were doing for training or caused guys to rethink how we trained to prepare for the inevitability of a gunfight. Plenty of guys looked to different areas for techniques or tactics as a solution to this new information about actual gunfights. I remember having my first discussion about what I call "hard skills" around 2004. In my mind, it proved that despite what we did in terms of tactics, techniques, or procedures, being fast and accurate with our primary weapons was now more important than ever. Developing my hard skills to the highest level became the focus of my training, and it continues to be to this day.

I first met Ben Stoeger in May 2013 at a range in Wisconsin. Prior to that, I cold-called him and discussed the possibility of training with him at his home range for a week. We briefly discussed his availability and what it would take to have his time for the week, and I asked him for an address to ship ammo to. Two days prior to our agreed-upon date, 5,000 rounds showed up at his house. On the first day of training, we met up at 7:00 a.m. and were shooting by 8:00 a.m. My very first impression of Ben, outside of his technical skill, was his ability to describe techniques in ways I could understand. I quickly realized we understood and spoke the same language with regards to training.

Fast forward to December 2019, Ben agreed to come teach a competition-based class with me at a range near my house in North Carolina. I recommended he stay for a week after the class to do some rifle training with me. He had expressed some interest in this and stated he had never really shot AR-style rifles. After the first few days of training rifle with Ben, a theory I had about pistol shooting translating to rifle shooting was proven to be true, at least to me. Training Ben was probably one of the most enjoyable and easiest things I've done regarding training. We shot a series of drills and exercises that were very practical in nature and emphasized a balance of speed, control, and aggression. The distances we were training at were not typical distances you see in "tactical carbine" training (based on my experiences in my professional life).

After that week, Ben was able to perform skills at levels that were absolutely astounding. I am not easily impressed with shooting abilities, but this time I was. Ben - a world champion shooter - saw the importance of dryfiring pistols and was able to translate that work ethic to the training ideas I had about dryfiring rifles. He worked on all the dryfire homework I gave him that week, and the results showed as we progressed. When Ben left North Carolina, he was very interested in progressing his rifle game. This was also very interesting to me because I had gotten to see firsthand how Ben had changed pistol training paradigms at my place of work, and I believed he would be able to do the same thing with the rifle. This was proven to be true, and now the birth of Adaptive Rifle will make it available to everyone.

Matt Pranka - @xray.alpha.llc
https://www.xrayalpha.com/

That training session in 2019 was probably, in all reality, the inception of what would become Adaptive Rifle. Taking practical-based principles about shooting handguns and modifying them to fit in the context of rifle shooting is the next evolution of training. In my opinion, to say Adaptive Rifle will change the way people understand rifle training is an understatement. Having shot many of the drills laid out in this book and watched the evolution, I know this will reset how guys who work with a rifle view training and performance. Everyone who puts effort - true effort - into their training knows it takes work. The amount of work is usually underestimated, and many people take to it with very little understanding of where the end state is or should be. I believe this book will change that for a lot of people.

—Matt Pranka

ADAPTIVE RIFLE

Welcome to *Adaptive Rifle*. This book is a training manual that should guide you from rookie to competent with your practical rifle shooting. This material is structured in a way that if you have no prior experience doing "serious" firearms training, you will obtain the tools you need to get to where you want to be.

Serious firearms training is a regular activity. It is a part of your life that you practice on a routine basis. Most high-level competitive shooters train with their equipment on a near-daily basis in order to get their skills to the highest level possible. Dry training at home is the primary way this is accomplished.

If you have experience with prior training materials written by us, the material and presentation found in this book will be familiar. Although those books are geared towards shooting pistols, they do use the same structure as this book, so you'll find yourself right at home.

This book is the culmination of experience and knowledge shared between myself (Ben Stoeger), Joel Park, Matt Pranka, and many others.

Joel Park is an expert on rifle equipment and pistol training. He has helped write, organize, and illustrate this text. His attention to detail and open mind is invaluable to this project. He brings his pistol competition and teaching background, along with very good technical knowledge about rifles.

Matt Pranka has a long career in Special Operations, a talent for shooting and an interest in getting better. Matt took the training system Ben used to win championships in the pistol world and adapted it to help him push his carbine shooting to the highest level possible.

In the years Ben has spent collaborating with Matt, they have both learned a lot. This manual is the product of much of what Ben has learned from him. Applying sport shooting training techniques into rifle shooting in order to shoot as aggressively as possible out to 75 yards or so and be able to hit man-sized targets at 400 yards is what this text is all about.

There are countless other individuals that contributed to this work. New ideas aren't generated very often in the shooting community. Typically, ideas are just regurgitated in different ways. This book interprets many old ideas in some fresh and different ways and in doing so tries to bring something new to the table.

UNDERSTANDING TRAINING

I have worked as a full-time shooting instructor for quite a long time. It's been more than a decade at the time of this writing. I meet lots of people. Most people I meet like the idea of training and improving more than they like the idea of actually training.

I have taught thousands of students in classes. I am always interested in what happens after the class is done. Most people who take a class walk away with a few things they want to work on, but in most cases, life gets in the way, and they never really implement the training they wanted to. This is very typical. I'm not criticizing those people; it's just the pattern I see.

Let's just say Matt was not one of these typical cases.

When I met Matt, I immediately recognized that he was very talented at shooting. Even more so, he was willing to work. His goal was a Grand Master (GM) ranking in USPSA. I could see that he had the raw talent and the drive to make it happen. He just needed a little bit of direction.

I should point out that it is very common for me to meet shooters that want to make GM. It is common for me to meet people that have the physical ability to make it. It is very uncommon for me to meet someone that wants it and is actually willing to do what it takes to make it happen.

I assessed his shooting at the time as accurate and safe. Matt needed some work moving around stages better. He needed to tune up his gun handling. I think mostly he just needed to see what was possible and understand how to train. His type A motivation to train would take care of the rest.

Over the course of that week, I showed Matt the training system I used for handguns. I showed him everything. The livefire par times I trained to, the accuracy standards, the technique, the dryfire. Really, I showed him everything we had time for.

We went through things in quite a lot of detail. Every dimension of shooting was broken down and assessed at a variety of target distances. This was several charts worth of information and dozens of drills with specific time standards.

This isn't the first time I have done this with someone, but it is definitely one of the more successful weeks of training I have had. Matt really "got it." In just a few months, Matt met his goal and earned a GM ranking in USPSA, and he was ready to move on to the next goal.

What really happened with Matt in that week was that a guy who is motivated, smart, and trainable was given the tools he needed to get where he wanted to go. As soon as Matt understood what areas to train and how to train them, it was inevitable that he would earn a GM card at some point.

This was just my first experience with Matt. I have known him for years and the knowledge has been flowing in both directions for a long time.

TRANSLATING PISTOL TO RIFLE

In Matt's introduction, he described this theory about shooting development; how developing strong pistol skills sets you up to be excellent with a carbine. It is frequently the case that a strong rifle shooter can't shoot a pistol that well, but the reverse is often not the same. Pistol shooters have the ability to adapt and become strong rifle shooters.

There are many reasons for training with handguns. Marksmanship issues with the pistol are much easier to see because it is much harder to shoot a pistol aggressively without the inclination to overcompensate for the recoil. Consider shooting from the 5-yard line with a 9mm Glock. This is certainly enough distance to understand a lot about your grip and other habits. These issues take a lot more distance to be exposed with a rifle.

A few years ago, I had almost zero experience with long guns. I was a perfect candidate for Matt to test his theory on. However, I was not the typical shooter. I was a world champion with a handgun, and I already understood training pretty well. Everyone says that long guns are "easier," so I figured I would be fine.

According to Matt's theory, I should have been able to apply my mechanical skills from pistol shooting to rifle shooting and become competent or even good with a rifle very quickly. My experience doing fast dryfire training with my handgun would inform me on how to practice with the rifle. I should be able to get pretty good very quickly with a rifle.

So, we set to work. After a week with Matt, I saw he had a pretty good grasp on what metrics he thought were important. For example, we had a table of goal times for the "standard practice setup" from competition pistol shooting. This is a setup that is popularized by having a battery of drills that can be run on three USPSA targets set up in a line. Matt had tested all his rifle times against those pistol drills, so he had a very good amount of data to work from.

When I was shooting rifles with Matt that first week, I must admit I felt like a fish in water. Everything I was doing was familiar: dryfire drills with strict par times, livefire drills with rigid enforcement of accuracy standards, and so forth. The gun I was using was totally different, but the familiarity of drills gave me a sense of doing a familiar job with an unfamiliar tool.

Matt had figured out par times for all the relevant dryfire drills. He knew the times for the live drills. He had really worked out adapting the pistol training drills we use in practical shooting to his carbine shooting.

The first week was instructive for me. It showed me a lot of things I wanted to improve on. It also showed that a good pistol shooter could absolutely apply those skills and become adept with a rifle pretty quickly. Since that first week I started training with a long gun, I have continued my training and continued to refine the technique and drills.

In the time since we started bouncing ideas off each other, I have done a lot of training and experimentation. Drills and concepts have been added to this material as we extensively tested them. It is my thinking that Adaptive Rifle will get tested and refined by the shooting community over the coming years. This system will be much improved in five years due to getting it to the masses.

REAL-WORLD EXPERIENCE

If you have something to train for, it obviously helps you organize your efforts in a productive way. Many people don't believe they can achieve that much on their own. If they put their mental energy to work in the right ways, they can absolutely achieve a lot.

All my "training" prior to competition was from books and magazine articles. I learned techniques, drills, and practice methods from the texts of the day. Even though I and many others offer classes, you don't need to take a class in order to improve. If you use this material and apply yourself, you can absolutely build world-class skills on your own.

In my case, one of the first performance challenges that I experienced was making "Master" in the IDPA classifier. In the years since, the classifier itself and the classification system have changed quite a bit. At the time, Master was the highest rank, and the classifier stage was a relatively complicated test requiring 90 rounds of ammo.

To prepare myself for competitive shooting, I took a couple of months and broke down the classifier match to understand all the components. I did drills to train on each part, and I set realistic goals for each piece of the classifier. This organization and goal helped me set a specific standard of training.

Even though I trained on my own with no instruction, minimal ammo and no relevant experience, the structure of my training worked.

Within a couple of months my skills had grown considerably, and I was able to make "Master" rank in IDPA at my first competitive shooting event. For me, I never needed more proof that individual training at home (dryfire), along with occasional range sessions, could make you extremely proficient with a firearm.

Like myself, Matt utilizes systematic training in order to accomplish his goals. Matt developed a widely used concept on how to assess your own performance on various exercises. Matt proposes that there are really three metrics to pay attention to when it comes to any shooting test: what is acceptable, what is good, and what is possible.

These concepts change quite a lot based on who you are and what you are trying to accomplish. A 1.5-second draw from the holster to hit a target at 7 yards is not very fast in the competitive shooting world. However, if you are hitting that time after a couple of weeks of owning a holster and starting to practice, you are doing just fine.

To give the exercises in this book some structure, the drills are organized around passing a relatively complicated test. CQB (Close Quarters Battle) Warmup is a test Matt designed and it requires 48 rounds to complete. Even the guys Matt worked with in the military need to be on their game to pass the test. This is the test that this book is organized around.

JOEL'S JOURNEY TO RIFLES

I have enjoyed shooting rifles since an early age. Before I discovered action pistol shooting, I did lots of slow-fire target shooting at various ranges focused on the best accuracy I could produce with ammo I carefully reloaded one round at a time. I bought a carbine and had shot it some, but any time I took it to the range I was focused on how accurately I could shoot it.

Fast forward to 2020, while Ben and I were already teaching classes together and constantly discussing training and teaching, my friends Kenny, Jon, Lane, and I decided to give local 2-gun matches a try. The first match was an eye-opener. I had glimpses of what was possible, but I was shooting nowhere near my potential. I didn't like not being the best at my club, so I started doing some infrequent training with my rifle. As I shot more 2-gun matches, I analyzed my performance to see the areas I was lacking in, and I started isolating skills and training in the same manner I was with handguns.

Since Ben had already done some rifle training with Matt, we started comparing notes on technique and observations we had made while shooting. Ben isn't a gear guy, and he didn't have any opinions about how a carbine should be set up. I decided I didn't like the way my rifle was configured, so I turned to my friends Kenny and Jon for help. Over the next year or so, I changed something on my rifle every few months as I developed preferences and learned how all the components affected each other. I continued to test my abilities in matches and training as the equipment changes became less and less frequent.

For Ben's first set of carbines, he sent me a picture of one of Matt's rifles and asked me to set up two guns to match the picture. He wasn't concerned about the details of what they were. At the beginning of 2022, Ben told me he wanted a second set of rifles. By then I had a stronger opinion of the setup I liked and had compared my findings with some high-level shooters. I insisted on Ben discussing the details of setting up the guns, much to his dismay. I explained my preference on parts that affected how the rifles behaved, such as moving to A2 flash hiders from the compensators he had on his previous rifles. We discussed how certain carbine builds can mask inefficiencies and how critical the fundamentals are to be able to perform at a high level with a basic rifle. This caused us to closely examine our techniques as we strived to get the best performance possible from a duty-style rifle.

Since then, we've learned a lot and continue to apply the same principles we use in handgun training to evolve how we train with rifles and what we view as possible.

—Joel Park

USING THIS BOOK

This book is organized to give you the training tools you need to succeed. We recommend you look through the entire book before you get started.

There is always a balancing act regarding how much material and what ideas to include in a book like this. A book detailing all sorts of special techniques and equipment considerations is not the objective here. We want this text to give you the required training information and answer some basic equipment/technique questions. That's it. The uncomfortable truth is that until you are competent in dealing with the drills and exercises in this book, more gear/technique knowledge isn't going to help you shoot better. You actually need to put in the time during dryfire to build your skills.

Please read through the technical pointers and equipment setup section. This should help get you and your gear ready for training. With diligent dryfire and careful use of your ammo, you should be able to make huge progress with one or two thousand rounds.

After that, make sure you have the key things needed for training. You will need an area where you can safely dryfire. You will need targets in that area. A shot timer is absolutely crucial as well. Once you get these essential things sorted out, you should be ready to start training.

This book is organized around helping you meet and exceed the standard set by CQB Warmup. This test will require fast and accurate shooting. It will also require you to be proficient with gun manipulations such as reloads and transitions. Shooting a passing score on CQB Warmup isn't an easy thing to do, especially if you are coming to this material without competition or training experience. It is a very good and achievable objective for a "regular" guy, and we recommend you make it your goal.

As you work through the drills in the book, understand that each drill has a dryfire workup associated with it. Most of your time is going to be spent doing this dryfire homework to prepare you for a good performance on the drills during your livefire.

Good luck with your training.

TRAINING

If you are interested in building exceptional skills, you need to train. Training is committing resources over time in order to improve. This means that if you want to fundamentally improve your rifle shooting, you need to put in the necessary time, energy, ammo, and so forth. This isn't something that can happen in a day, a week, or even a month. Effective training takes serious time and effort.

Many people have the idea in their head that if they simply do whatever it is they want to be good at, then eventually they will get good at that thing. People think that if they do competitive shooting for a certain amount of time, they will get where they want to go. This is not the case. Simply committing time to this endeavor will not make you proficient. To be honest, it takes something more.

Real training is about putting in the time and reps while you pay attention to what is happening. You can't just go through the motions and do the drills as the procedure says. That isn't good enough. There needs to be a process of assessment and analysis. You need to get your brain involved with what is going on.

Slowly, your conscious mind changes subconscious habits into muscle memory as you do repetitions. Your training will require repetitions to build these subconscious habits as you work your way through drills.

Daily Habit

Before we go too far down the training rabbit hole, it is important to understand the proper mindset for training. The most productive and effective firearms training happens when you start to make it a daily (or near-daily) habit. You will progress very quickly if you work at it a little bit each day.

People get the idea in their heads that in order to become proficient at shooting, they can just go to the range and shoot a bunch of ammo on a Saturday. They think they can take a weekend class with instructors like us, and that will fix all of their problems. It really doesn't work that way.

The most effective training will be mental. You need to build a mindset of daily thought, attention, and effort. You need that focus to be a better shooter. You can take a class or read a book to give you some insight and direction, but you need to realize that training needs to be an ongoing process.

The most successful shooters we know work at their shooting (with either livefire or dryfire) almost every day. It is as simple as that. If you want to be scary good at shooting, you are going to need to put in some serious time.

The dryfire areas in our homes have dummy magazines and belt setups that are ready to go. There are targets that are set up for us to train with. We have timers and grip chalk on a table. The convenience makes it easier for us to train. This is not by accident. It needs to be a part of our lives, and the easier it is to fit it into our lives, the more likely we are to follow through. When you don't make something easy to do, you are creating barriers for yourself and an easy excuse to not complete the task at hand.

Inductive Training

Conventional firearms training is (by definition) the normal method that people use to become proficient with firearms. This style of training focuses on safety and slow fire marksmanship. When those things are understood by the student, then the speed and complexity of the shooting challenges is slowly increased over time.

The student usually hits a plateau in their ability with this type of training. Commonly, this plateau happens when you need to start "cheating" or breaking rules to go faster. We don't mean breaking safety rules; we mean breaking rules about how the sight picture should look for each shot. Eventually, you need to start learning how to do more with less of a sight picture.

Conventional training for firearms certainly has its place. Learning fundamental safety and marksmanship rules is absolutely necessary to become a proficient shooter. However, there are limits to how far this can take you. Eventually, you will become proficient and level off in terms of ability. You will not get better without pushing yourself.

Inductive training is a core component of this book. With inductive training, you will be working within a time limit to shoot a drill. This uncomfortably paced shooting will certainly contribute to a lot of mistakes, but you will also quickly learn the cause of these mistakes (as long as you are paying attention).

Think of inductive training as purposefully exceeding your skill limits in a safe and controlled manner. You can then use the information that you learn from your failures to start succeeding.

This book asks you to meet a certain pace which is a firm - but fair - challenge. If you train hard, you will achieve a lot this way.

"Don't criticize mistakes; analyze them." One of Ben's business partners, Hwansik Kim, gave him that advice once and it bears mention. As you advance in this book and start going really fast, you will definitely make mistakes. Don't waste your time criticizing yourself; instead, just rationally analyze what happened. What did you see? What did you experience? If you search through your sensations while you are shooting faster than you are generally capable of, you will learn quite a lot about what needs to happen to get you to improve. A common result is that people learn how to round corners and do things sooner rather than faster. Perhaps you stop to analyze why you keep failing at fast rifle reloads and you notice you are trying to insert the magazine at the wrong angle. Maybe you notice your hand placement on the spare magazine is constantly changing every time you remove it from your mag pouch. Paying attention to the details can help you correct errors faster than just repping it out for 30 minutes, hoping it will improve.

Timers

One invaluable tool that all serious shooters use is a shot timer. For those unfamiliar with shot timers, let us take a moment to explain what they are.

The primary purpose of a shot timer is to record the time from a start signal (usually audible) to the last shot fired. The timer gets this information by hearing the gunshots through a microphone.

The timer also measures the time between gunshots. These are referred to as "split times." This information can be broken down and analyzed in detail to provide you with information about both your absolute skill level and the relative strengths and weaknesses of your shooting.

For example, a common split time to be interested in is the shot-to-shot time for a reload. If you are shooting an exercise that includes a reload, you can scroll through the timer and check that specific split time. This information allows you to direct your training in the most productive way possible.

This book includes some detailed metrics for appropriate split times for a variety of different things. These times change based on the target distances, the circumstances, and having a sense of what is "good" and what is "bad."

If you buy into the training methodology outlined in this book, you will be using a timer just as much for dry training as live training. Most timers have a "par" function that allows you to set a specific time limit. Let's say you want a 1.8-second par time. This means that a start beep will sound to start the drill. After 1.8 seconds have elapsed, a second beep will sound, indicating that the time limit has been reached.

The par function allows you to set a timeframe to work within to accomplish a task. It gives you the push you need in dryfire to get faster. It allows you to have some sense of how fast you are going.

If you haven't previously used a timer, you should understand that time is a big dimension of your shooting. Anyone can shoot accurately. Anyone can shoot fast. Few can do both at the same time. If you aren't using a timer, you will not be fast.

Dryfire

Dry training is training with your real firearm, but not using any ammunition. Many shooters who have not done regular training with their firearms think dryfire is limited to pointing your gun at a spot and slowly pressing the trigger so that nothing moves as you release the shot. This is a very limited view of what can be accomplished in dryfire.

As far as we are concerned, you can work on every element of your shooting in dryfire except for returning the gun from recoil. You need to spend live ammunition to get acclimated to how the gun moves under recoil. You also need to shoot some live ammunition to validate that you are dryfiring correctly. At the end of the day, most of your actual training can be done without ammunition.

The normal training paradigm that we preach to people is that they should do limited livefire in order to validate their dryfire and to understand where to take their dryfire next. The dry repetition is actually considered to be the real training.

The reason that dryfire is considered the primary type of training is economic as well as practical. Dryfire can be done in your home on a daily basis. If you are diligent with your self-assessment, you will improve very quickly.

Dryfire is basically the only way to get the reps and the frequency required to get really good, really fast. Unless you happen to have a job that gets you on a shooting range every day, you are going to need to dryfire regularly. Most people don't even have the option of shooting at the range every week, so this is the only way they can consistently practice.

If you don't already have a dryfire space in your home, you should create one. You don't need all the stuff we mentioned having in our spaces, but it is necessary to have a space that has a safe backstop (such as a basement). We recommend setting up scaled miniature targets and doing your training in that space. We suggest keeping all live ammunition out of that space. The use of dummy rounds is also encouraged so you can train more realistically and so that the magazines will weigh the same as they will on the range.

It is also important to point out that you can do dryfire at the range as well. When you set up a livefire training session, you should warm up with your dryfire before you start spending bullets trying to improve yourself.

Lasers, airsoft, sim guns, etc., are all useful training tools in some way. These ancillary tools mostly offer you some sort of fun or different way to train. If you get engaged with one of these things and it helps you, that's great. However, none of these tools will replace dry training with your actual firearm. Using tools such as airsoft guns is interesting for training, but really it's best to get used to your real firearm and train with that.

Dryfire Procedure (ABCs of a session)

If you do get into the habit of daily or near-daily dryfire, this is how we recommend you do it.

Select a few drills to work on each day. Two to four is a pretty good number that works for a lot of people. It is counterproductive to train past the point of focus, so it is important not to spend too much time dryfiring in a deliberate or slow sort of way. You should do a more limited number of very aggressive repetitions that you assess very rigidly. Most people cannot keep this up for more than 15-20 minutes. As soon as mental or physical fatigue sets in, you should stop.

If you spend three to five minutes doing rep after rep on a drill, you will be pretty well exhausted after that 15-20-minute timeline. Again, you need to have a very harsh and honest assessment about what you are seeing and doing. You do not want to train yourself to hold your gun incorrectly or too softly. You don't want to be training to use the wrong aiming scheme on the wrong target type, etc. Dryfire doesn't give you the feedback that live ammo does. This means that if you get sucked into wishful thinking about your dryfire, thinking that you are doing everything right when you aren't, you are going to be in for a rude awakening when you do live training. If you are happy with the majority of the reps you are doing, your dryfire practice is not being done correctly. You need to have a very high level of focus that is constantly looking for something that could be done better for every single repetition.

Here's an example of a dryfire session:

Practice bringing your rifle up from the hunt position (rifle stock shouldered, sights below eye line, safety on) to a target and having the sights stop exactly how you want them to for three to five minutes. Use a variety of target types and difficulties. Make sure you are using the correct aiming scheme and staying relaxed.

Work on target transitions for three to five minutes. Get the appropriate sight picture on each target you are using. Ensure the gun moves precisely to your aimpoints on each target. Pay attention to how the sights stop and where they land on the targets. Make sure your eyes move before the sights do. Try to increase the speed and see if you can do so without sacrificing accuracy.

Train magazine changes for three minutes. Do 20 reps grabbing the magazine from your pouch and bringing it to the magwell, then start doing the entire reload. Use a tight par time on the timer to hold yourself accountable with the speed. Make sure when you grab the magazine and bring it to the gun, your movements are fast and consistent. Make sure you are seating the magazines without tapping

on them more than once, and the mags are being fully seated while they are full of dummy rounds.

Train transitions from rifle to pistol for three minutes. Attempt to match your draw time (with just your pistol) with your transition time. Make sure you minimize "noise" in your movements, such as unneeded body movement or leaning. Any extra motion will slow things down, so make sure that isn't happening.

At the end of working on those four drills your hands should feel tired, and you will likely be ready for a break. Try to assess everything that happened and make sure to include the areas you struggled with in your next dryfire practice session.

Range Training

This book doesn't require a whole lot in the way of equipment.

All that is really needed to effectively utilize the drills in this book are stands for a few targets and the ability to shoot in a 180-degree arc. Being able to shoot at least 50 yards is important, so make sure your range has the ability for you to do that. Of course, being able to shoot further is always better.

What we recommend for your range training is that you select two or three drills from this book and go put some rounds into them. We recommend lots of repetition on a simple set of drills, rather than trying to do 10 different things and only one or two repetitions of each thing. More repetition on the same drill allows you to notice patterns and correct them.

As you work through a drill, we recommend doing three to five repetitions before you assess the target. This allows you to spot mistakes that appear often without tunneling your attention onto very infrequent issues or minor problems. If you force yourself to look at the larger picture of your shooting, you will no doubt improve a lot faster. Try to zoom out and look at the results for the entire practice session.

Reading the patterns of repeated mistakes is the most important part of your range training. You can start fixing those mistakes during your dry training. Examples of patterns could be sporadic hits on a target due to not picking an appropriate aiming scheme, hits clustering in an incorrect area on the target due to not finding the center of the target, or lots of low and left hits caused by pushing into the gun while you fire.

Livefire Procedure (ABCs of a session)

We recommend range sessions consisting of 100-200 rounds with your rifle. If you mix in dryfire while on the range (as you should), this amount of ammo will last 60-90 minutes and should make for a productive session. You shouldn't need a lot of ammunition to make a lot of progress.

Doing two different drills in a range session seems to be a good number for most people. It can be very productive if the drills you select aren't related so you can test multiple aspects of your shooting. If you are practicing a drill that requires running, like Go Stop or 80 to 10, we recommend the second drill be something you can do stationary.

While you are practicing the drills, you should be validating what you thought was happening in your dryfire practice. Having a very rigid assessment of your technique is important because your livefire informs your dryfire, and the reverse is also true. One form of training has ammo and the other does not, but fundamentally dryfire and livefire should be the same with respect to the level of focus and effort you use.

Bouncing back and forth between dryfire and livefire while on the range is also something you should be doing. If you notice a target transition issue you want to fix, there would be little need to spend ammo while you work on moving the sights to the spot you want to hit. The same is true for anything related to gun handling or getting in and out of positions. Save that ammo while you work on the skill dry, then test what you think is happening with live ammo to validate your training.

Whether you are a multiple-time champion or a novice shooter, this method of training is the way to go. It will produce the best result with the lowest number of resources.

Training Plan

You should establish and commit to a regular plan for your training. As we previously discussed, the core part of your training should be dry repetition at home. Dry training three or more days a week will give you very rapid improvement in your skill. If you can spend more time, it will be even better.

A dry training session can easily be only 10 or 15 minutes a day. As long as you are working on very specific skills and you are rigidly assessing the outcome of your drills, you are going to improve very quickly. The more days you put in work like that, the better.

Remember, it is better to be extremely critical and attentive for a shorter dryfire session than it is to do a longer dryfire session where you are just going through the motions. Be very critical in your assessment and you will benefit.

We recommend live training every week or two if you are really serious. This will give you plenty of dryfire time to onboard changes that you need to make based on your previous livefire training. Think about how your live training will feed your ideas for your dry training and keep yourself motivated. That's exactly the kind of feedback loop we think you should encourage.

To quote our friend Andreas Yankopolus, "People overestimate how much they can accomplish in a day, but they underestimate how much they can accomplish in a year." We can't emphasize this enough. Developing a sustainable training plan that works with your schedule is absolutely essential. Even if your schedule only allows for training two or three days a week, you will be shocked at how much you can accomplish.

Potential Paths

If you are coming to this book with some experience training with firearms, timers, etc., we think the best way to move forward is to go out and shoot CQB Warmup for a score. It is recommended to shoot it cold (no practice at the range beforehand with live ammo). This cold shooting assessment will give you a really good idea about where you stand.

When you shoot CQB Warmup, note your score and time for each string of fire. Early on, it is best to inspect the targets between each string, so you know exactly where each bullet went. Note the times as well. Make sure you are getting the shots off in the required time for each string. Remove five points from your score for each shot more than 0.30 seconds over the par time.

CQB Warmup should give you a good idea about your weak spots. Your speed and precision will be tested, as well as your firearm manipulations. The fast 40-yard shooting and the fast manipulations at the 7- and 10-yard lines are likely going to be the weak points for most people.

Once you discover your weak points using CQB Warmup, you can focus on your live and dry training efforts to improve those areas to get you up to the standard you want to be. Being able to consistently pass CQB Warmup is a pretty good goal.

If you are new to serious training, you shouldn't go straight to CQB Warmup. Instead, we recommend you take it from the top. Work through all the drills and concepts in this book in a systematic fashion to make sure you understand them. When you have practiced a bit and worked your way through the drills, go give CQB Warmup a try and see where you fall short. Find those weak points and work on them. If you make a constant effort to improve over time, you will make gains. Tracking your scores and times on the drills in this book can help you keep track of your progress, and it can really help motivate you as well. It is difficult to feel like you are improving when the gains are so marginal on a day-to-day basis. However, if you keep track of your scores and times, you will have a good set of data to refer back to. This will give you a real perspective on your shooting.

A second branching point that occurs for almost every shooter is whether you are predisposed for raw speed or accuracy. There aren't a lot of shooters who start out being fast and accurate. Some shooters are wired for very strict accuracy and they're willing to sacrifice speed to guarantee the accuracy they want. Other shooters might always have the need for speed, and consistently produce very fast times, but have lots of misses or loose hits.

Learning how you are wired and what makes you tick is an important part of training. You may find it helpful to create rules for yourself, such as making sure you see appropriate sight pictures before firing to clean up your accuracy, or not waiting for the perfect sight picture before firing to gain speed.

If you pay attention, you will learn how to get the best performance from yourself as you train more and more. You'll learn how to direct the thoughts and feelings you have during your training as well. This is a process that takes place over time. This book is just a road map to help you build proficiency. If you dedicate yourself to steady effort, you are going to learn a lot and be able to meet any reasonable standard.

FOCUS

It is important to understand that the ideas you put inside of your head are going to affect the outcome you get.

This is true in every dimension of your life, but our focus is on training here.

The most important thing you can do as a shooter is manage where you put your attention. This may sound strange at first, but stick with us and it will be productive.

First, you have to understand a few basic things:

1. Your conscious mind is your objective or thinking mind. It has no memory, and it can only hold one thought at a time.
2. Where you put your mind will have a big impact on what happens as you shoot.
3. As you observe your shooting, you will learn where to focus your attention for the best results.

Perception of shooting changes for each individual and how they react to different circumstances. Learning to shoot better doesn't just take training and repetition. You will obviously need lots of ammo and time to get really good. You will need to engage your mind with your training to discover how to reach your potential. Shooting is not an easy thing to sort out, and your body will probably not cooperate with you all the time. It isn't just about "repping it out." Perform repetitions while you are mentally engaged.

Sometimes you might think "go faster" and what your body hears is "tense up." This is a huge fundamental problem for people in their training. Most shooters need to spend a lot of time evaluating what outputs their body gives them based on psychological inputs. It isn't an easy task.

You might find that you need to focus on your wrist to stop yourself from driving the gun down in recoil. That is a pretty common situation, but you will not figure out if it applies to you without doing some experimentation.

Your brain doesn't always function in a way that you think is logical. For example, the more relaxed Ben can get his firing hand to hold onto his .40 caliber Limited Division guns, the faster and better he can shoot. His perception is that he is barely gripping the gun. However, if you look at what is happening under a high-speed camera, you can see that he is indeed holding the gun very firmly and it is only his perception telling him that he is barely holding the gun.

Your own perception of what is happening while you are doing high-speed shooting should not be trusted. You will lose your sense of muscle tension as well as your sense of time. You might feel very slow while performing a drill, but the timer says differently. This is very normal. You will need to carefully sort out each detail of what your body is doing to maximize your potential.

You should also consider that performance pressure will complicate the situation even further. Your perception of your shooting will change even more dramatically as the pressure stacks up. Real performance shooting is tested under real stress. There really isn't any alternative. If you don't do competitive shooting, you might experience some of this stress by trying CQB Warmup with some friends.

Once you accept the idea that what you are thinking about while you are training really affects the outcome, you will want to understand the inputs that you are putting in. Once you figure out the correct input, it is important to keep focused on it.

It takes weeks of repetitions with your conscious mind actively engaged on a specific cue to actually change a particular habit. If your focus wanders, it won't work. If you don't assess what you are doing - good or bad - you will never improve.

As you are training and sorting out your technique, ask yourself this: What is the correct cue for me to focus on?

The correct cue is the one that works. For example, you might have a problem overdriving the gun as you transition from target to target. We suggest the following cues as possible fixes for the problem:

- Look where you want to go and let the gun come to you.
- Allow your knees to bend as you transition around.

- Keep your upper body mount the same. Do not allow your support hand to push the rifle.
- Look at a coin-sized spot on the target you are transitioning to.

This is just a short list. The number of cues you could focus on are only limited by your imagination.

If we have a student with a target transition problem, we simply suggest cues that they focus on until one of the cues starts working. You can only focus on one thing at a time, so the idea here is that the student just tries different mental focal points until one of them starts working.

It doesn't matter if the cue sounds dumb or feels silly. Everyone's brain is wired a little bit differently and all these ideas are filtered through your own personal perception. We have seen guys focus on their pinky finger to get their hand pressure to cooperate. Whatever you choose to focus on doesn't matter; the right cue is the one that works.

Self-awareness is the key to improvement. The more you pay attention to what is happening, the more you will understand how to influence your shooting through your mental focus. Once you find the cues that work for you, put your focus on them one at a time during your training to alter your habits.

To bullet point this list:

- Push your shooting ability on drills/ tests.
- Assess/observe not just the time/score of your shooting, but what actually happened.

- Implement training one cue at a time - over time - in order to change your habits.
- Push your shooting ability on drills/ tests to assess the changes.
- Repeat this process over time using all training resources (time, ammo, etc.) you care to spend.

Intellectual Understanding vs. Cue

When we are teaching, we very frequently need to talk to people about understanding vs. cueing. It is one thing to understand what you should do in terms of technique, but having that understanding doesn't always correlate with what you actually do, especially when you are performing at speed and under pressure.

Students frequently make this mistake. They understand what they should do. They are shooting the drills in class and doing reps, trying to get better. The problem is that they don't actually focus on a specific cue during their shooting. They talk about what they are going to do and then shoot the drill differently than what they verbalized, but there doesn't seem to be much understanding of what just happened.

Shooting technique isn't about understanding what you are trying to do. You need to mindfully focus on a specific task during your shooting in order to change habits. You need to be consciously observing what is happening while you fire. This is required during the drill if you wish to complete the task.

It's about what happens during the drill, not before or after. It doesn't matter what you think you want to do or what you think you just did. Pay attention while the shooting is actually happening.

Trust your Subconscious

One concept people struggle with is conscious effort vs. subconscious proficiency.

As you train or do any task, you will build subconscious routines. Think about how you drive your car without conscious effort while you carry on a conversation with a passenger. Driving is second nature, and you don't need to think about what you are doing. You just put your foot on the pedal and drive.

Shooting training is similar in the sense that you will have many processes happening simultaneously. You should get comfortable with the idea that you don't consciously control every aspect of your shooting at all times. When you start going fast you will see that you can't work like that - nobody can. You can only control one element of your shooting at a time consciously. The element you control during training should be the element you are attempting to correct or change.

One challenge people face is accepting that most things need to be left to the subconscious. For example, a very common correction given when shooting the Practical Accuracy Drill is to increase support-side pressure on the gun and pull the gun straight back into your shoulder. Many students hear the correction, but then don't consciously implement it while they are shooting. They nod their heads and go right back to what they were previously doing on the drill.

These students aren't trying to be jerks or not listen; they listen and understand what they want to do and then shoot the drill again. They don't consciously take control of one aspect of their shooting by applying a cue. They don't really trust themselves to allow subconscious sight alignment while they put their brain on something else. Until you learn to cue properly, it's hard to change your habits.

Self-Awareness/Insight

Your ability to look at what you are doing from a very critical, but honest perspective is important for your development as a shooter. If your mind starts to wander during your training, it will be reflected in your results and your training won't be as effective. Doing reps over and over without really understanding why you are getting the results you're getting isn't very productive. Whether you are dryfiring at home or throwing rounds down range, if you are not self-aware of what is actually happening and what you are actually doing, you're not going to progress very quickly. Self-awareness is the key to improving. Being able to understand and see what is happening and why is a vital part of your training. That is why being mentally focused on the task at hand is so crucial.

EQUIPMENT

Rifle Setup Considerations

The majority of gun owners love talking about modifying their firearms. The internet is full of videos and articles about favorite load-outs and guns that are set up for the apocalypse. This book is designed for training with duty-style rifles, and we want to explain the thought process behind setting up our gear the way that we do.

This isn't meant to be a "you should buy this" guide, so if you already own something you really like or have something different issued to you, just use what you have. This is just a list of the stuff we currently use and like.

All of the Drills in this Book were Developed with the following:

Duty-style rifles with minimally compensated muzzle devices, two-stage triggers, unmagnified red dots, mid-length gas systems, Magpul B.A.D. levers and lowers that do not have competition magwells. These guns all fired 5.56 or .223 ammunition.

When using more competition-oriented muzzle devices, heavier guns, lighter triggers, etc., you will be able to push what is possible on these drills.

It is still possible to push these drills if you are using a mil-spec trigger and iron sights – it will just be harder. Be aware of the equipment considerations when shooting these drills.

Optics

Purpose dictates gear and people get very emotional about the red dot vs. low power variable optic (LPVO) discussion.

The drills in this book are designed to make you fast and accurate from very close range, out to 100 yards. For that application, red dot optics are preferred. There isn't much utility to an LPVO when shooting man-sized targets inside of 50 yards.

Other issues with LPVOs are reticle and eye relief/tube construction. Scope reticles are either first or second focal plane. First focal plane reticles change size to become larger as you increase the level of magnification, and second focal plane reticles stay the same regardless of magnification level. This in itself creates several headaches.

First focal plane reticles changing with the magnification means your drop/hold-overs will be the same regardless of which power setting you are on, which can be extremely helpful. The downside is that the reticle is typically not very impressive for fast shooting on 1x or the lower magnification settings but becomes very good on the higher magnification settings. Second focal plane reticles never change. If you create a chart for your holds, it will only be accurate on the specific magnification your chart is for, so the versatility isn't as good. The upside is that the reticles are typically far more useful on 1x and the lower magnification settings and are much better suited for fast, aggressive shooting.

The other main issue with LPVOs is the eye relief and what typically happens with your vision. Moving very aggressively, then shooting while decelerating is very tough with an LPVO due to the distance and height/alignment your eye needs with the scope before you can see through the tube. If you and the rifle are bouncing around, it can be very difficult to get a usable sight picture compared to just seeing a red dot on a piece of glass.

In a perfect world, all rifle shooting would be done while target focused, and that is difficult to do with an LPVO. Most shooters' eyes are drawn to the reticle regardless of the magnification setting, and they stare at the reticle while trying to move it to the target. This can also turn shooters into perfectionists that over aim while continually refining the sight picture past what is acceptable to make hits on the target.

Scopes are without question superior for long-range shooting and in a do-it-all role they might make sense. But for the purpose of this book, we are focused on fast, aggressive shooting from CQB distances out to 100 yards.

We use EOTech and Holosun optics that feature a 68/65 MOA ring and a small center dot. The reticle allows for several aiming schemes that are very easy to remember. The large 68/65 MOA ring can be used for fast, close-range shooting or just centering the circle on the target. The large ring can also be used as a way for you to locate the center dot

faster due to the proximity. The small center dot provides a very precise aiming scheme when shooting at small targets or longer distances. The ring also has a hash at the bottom, which is the offset for 7 yards (when the rifle is zeroed at 50/200 yards) and is extremely useful for precise shooting at close distances. We will expand on using different aiming schemes shortly.

The only negatives that we have experienced with red dots are that they can be tougher to shoot at longer ranges due to lack of magnification and can run out of batteries. Storing an extra set of batteries in the pistol grip or stock of your rifle is helpful.

Zero and Optic Height

We use a 50/200-yard zero, but whatever zero you prefer is fine. Be aware that different barrel lengths will produce different velocities, so a 50/200-yard zero might work with a 16" barrel but will be much different with a 10.5" barrel. More importantly, it is imperative to understand how height over bore affects where your bullets will go. The closer you get your optic to the barrel, the less variance there will be. Some equipment - such as night vision - encourages the use of optic risers. Regardless of what setup you choose, be aware of where the bullets hit at different ranges. This is just as important in close-range shooting as it is when shooting at distance.

Muzzle Device

The muzzle device has a large effect over how loud the rifle is and how much it recoils.

Intended application will dictate your decision. Compensators reduce recoil at the cost of a lot more muzzle blast and gas pushed to both sides of the shooter. They can be very unpleasant for someone standing next to you or when firing them in an enclosed space, but they can be very beneficial for some shooting sports. Suppressors add weight to the end of the gun and can make it more awkward to move around, but they have obvious sound reduction benefits. If you plan to use a suppressor, make sure you choose a compatible muzzle device.

We have found that basic A2 flash hiders give excellent performance when paired with solid fundamentals and a good mount. They are also very pleasant to use due to the lack of noise and blast compared to ported muzzle devices. The intended application is very important to consider when researching muzzle devices.

Trigger

For a duty-style rifle, light single-stage triggers are not recommended due to safety concerns regarding accidental discharges. Someone on the internet will chime in with a "my trigger finger is my safety" quote, but the reality is that a mil-spec or two-stage trigger can be shot just as well as a single-stage trigger.

We prefer using either an enhanced mil-spec trigger, or a two-stage trigger. A two-stage trigger is basically what it sounds like. The first stage has slack or take-up similar to a Glock trigger. The second stage starts at the wall and typically has a crisp break. For resetting the trigger, it only needs to move past the break at the second stage, before it can be pulled back to the wall for follow-up shots.

Anything in the Geissele/ALG Defense lineup is easy to recommend due to their track record and our experiences with them. If you are on a budget, the ALG Defense Advanced Combat Trigger is our go-to. It offers a much smoother and more predictable trigger over the factory standard mil-spec trigger that comes in most rifles. If budget allows, the Geissele SSA-E is another go-to. The SSA-E is a two-stage trigger that offers a safety net of a heavier first-stage pull before you get to a light break on the second stage.

Other triggers we like are the Geissele Super 3-Gun trigger, Super Dynamic Super 3-Gun trigger, SSA, and ALG Defense Quality Mil-Spec trigger. Lastly, you can get a lot accomplished with a basic mil-spec trigger. If that's what you have, do not feel like it's a limiting factor for improvement.

Stock Length

It is worth mentioning buttstock length of pull. If your rifle has an adjustable stock, a good rule of thumb is to place your hand on the pistol grip and extend the stock until it contacts your bicep. You may find it more comfortable moving the stock in or out from there, but that should give you a good starting point.

Sling

A sling is basically a holster for your rifle and is considered an essential piece of gear. We use two-point slings, and there are lots of good options available. The features we look for are ease of use and adjustment, with minimal clutter or unwanted things getting in the way. We prefer the Edgar Sherman Design ESD sling or the T.REX Arms sling due to their ease of use and adjustment options.

There are a lot of options for mounting slings on most rifles. We use QD mounts and suggest you try different options to see what works best for you. The most popular configurations are using a mounting point just forward of the receiver, attached to the forearm, paired with either the end of the buttstock or a mounting plate behind the receiver just under the castle nut.

There are a few things to evaluate when testing different sling setups, and supporting gear comes into play as well. With your regular rig/kit on, make sure you can do all the different loading, unloading and gun handling things you might want to do. Make sure you can lock the bolt to the rear, even if you don't plan on needing to. If you are training with a handgun, make sure your sling allows you to move the rifle out of the way enough to access a full grip on your handgun.

Tuning Your Rifle

Barrel length typically dictates what length of gas system your rifle is set up with. The most common styles are carbine- and mid-length gas systems. Regardless of muzzle device, shorter barreled rifles using carbine-length gas systems operate more violently while offering a more compact package. Rail space also comes at a premium since there is less room to mount accessories. Shorter barrels are also preferred for most suppressor use. Longer barrels will offer more bullet velocity, less noise, and the longer mid-length gas system for a more pleasant shooting rifle, but that comes at a cost of weight and size.

Different weight buffers are an easy way to change the recoil impulse of your rifle. The most common are the Carbine, H1, H2, and H3 buffers. Most manufacturers have a recommendation based on barrel length and gas system. Adding a heavier buffer will often make the recoil feel softer.

For an unsuppressed carbine, we prefer 13.7-16" barrels with a mid-length gas system, H2 buffer, and a flash hider-style muzzle device. The result is a rifle that is very pleasant to shoot in terms of recoil and noise/blast.

Accessories

Other accessories we use are Magpul B.A.D. levers which allow you to manipulate the bolt catch without removing your firing hand from the grip. They speed up bolt lock reloads and allow you to lock the bolt open with your firing hand very easily. We would consider them almost essential for any right-handed shooter that regularly trains.

Enhanced charging handles just make life easier for manipulations and add much more surface area to grab for clearing stoppages. There are a variety of really good options that boil down to personal preference. We like the charging handles made by Radian Weapons and Geissele.

Weapon-mounted flashlights are a necessity for most work/duty-style rifles. There are a lot of companies making quality lights and a plethora of mounting solutions and activation options. We're not experts with any tactic that involves using a light, but we have two key things we think are worth mentioning. First, make sure the activation is something you can do intuitively from your normal shooting grip - something you need to search for will not do the trick. Secondly, move the light towards the muzzle/suppressor to minimize/eliminate the shadow your muzzle creates. Several companies create products for moving lights towards the muzzle, such as T.REX Arms, Arisaka Defense, and Haley Strategic Partners.

Lefty Setup

A few bolt-on parts can make a stock carbine user friendly for a left-handed shooter. Joel is left-handed and uses an ambidextrous safety and charging handle at a bare minimum. He prefers the Geissele Super Configurable Safety Selector because the user can decide which length they would like the short or long safety paddle on. It can be set with the short side on the left side of the receiver, so it's not rubbing on your trigger finger while shooting.

Other products that have proven to be helpful are the Troy Industries Ambidextrous Magazine Release and the Geissele Maritime Bolt Catch. The Troy Industries release allows releasing the magazine with your trigger finger, so it's possible to reload the rifle just as fast as a right-handed shooter. The Maritime Bolt Catch extends the bolt catch towards the grip and allows the bolt to be locked open and released with the trigger finger. It's not quite as easy as using a Magpul B.A.D. Lever, but it makes the rifle very usable for fast gun handling.

TECHNIQUE

This technique section is designed to give you the "how" behind the "what" contained in the drills section. It is important to read this section very closely in order to build a solid understanding of what the techniques herein are intended to accomplish. The ideas that you train yourself to implement matter a lot. The way that you conceptualize the techniques in this book is so critical that it can't be overstated.

The fact is that if you have a counterproductive idea about technique, it will hold you back. Let us give you an example:

When training people for competitive pistol shooting, we often run into iron sight shooters that insist on seeing a perfect "equal height, equal light" sight picture before every single shot. If the students have mastered a clean trigger press at that pace, they end up stacking rounds on top of one another, but doing so at such a slow pace basically makes it irrelevant.

These shooters master a technique, but that technique will only be good for very distant/difficult targets. There are much faster methods for engaging closer targets.

You have to apply honesty and introspection to your shooting as you try to apply these concepts. Many people believe they are "learning" something just by reading it in a book, but the real learning comes in practical application.

Read through things carefully, go try some live training and do some dryfire. Then reread the technique section and carefully think about what you are actually seeing and doing, rather than what you know you are trying to do.

Most shooters struggle to stay focused on a small spot on the target. If they recognize that this is a struggle, they usually work on the issue and improve it. If they read "be target focused" in a book but never critically assess their own shooting, they will just believe they are target focused.

The same thing happens when it comes to properly mounting your rifle, exercising good trigger control, doing aggressive dryfire, and so forth.

The bottom line is that this technical stuff is very difficult. Trying to actually get yourself to do it properly at speed is more difficult. Read it carefully. Try it. Read it again. Assess. Don't take anything for granted. These concepts seem simple, but they are very difficult to implement at speed under pressure.

PERMISSION TO FAIL

The most common way people are taught to shoot is very accuracy-centric. This is good for several legal and professional reasons. When you train police officers or soldiers, you need to make sure they are safe and can hit a target. Once that minimum baseline is set, you can go from there.

You will find that once you get a shooter to the point where they are safe and can predictably hit targets while following certain marksmanship "rules," they tend to develop to the point where their understanding of the rules holds them back. Shooting with your dot stopped and centered for every shot will get you hits every time but will hold you back in terms of speed. People need to be pushed to go faster in order to understand and overcome their limitations.

Specifically, what people need is permission to fail. Permission to try to go faster and not always connect with the target. The purpose of this is to learn why you are missing when you go fast. Don't think of it as training yourself to miss; it is an opportunity for you to learn from the misses. Every single top-level shooter fired many misses on the way to mastery, because it is the only way to learn how to connect speed and accuracy.

Most of the material in this book is intended to be worked on extensively. The things you are asked to do are challenging. These drills take training to perform and

dedicated practice to master. You are going to fail many times on the road to succeeding.

You want to push yourself within the bounds of comfort and safety. Don't go so fast that you are shooting in an unsafe direction or losing control of the gun. You should push yourself to get comfortable shooting quickly, though.

The rule we use when pushing ourselves is this: If we can see and understand where the shots went, then we are fine. When we go downrange and we genuinely don't know where the shots went, then we are pushing too hard or not paying attention.

The key is for you to pay attention to the problems you encounter as you push yourself, not the result. For example, if you are shooting CQB Warmup and you can't shoot a score above 190 under the time limits, examine why. Once you really understand your weak points, you can work on solving them.

Open up your senses when you are training. Pay attention to the tension that you feel in your body as you are shooting aggressively. Some of it will be productive and some of it counterproductive. The behavior of the gun and dot during your shooting should help you connect cause (your inputs into the gun) with effect (where the bullets go).

When you can understand and articulate what is happening, you will be able to fix the problem. For example: "I need to shoot less

Charlies. My shooting is too wild." This statement lacks specificity. What are you actually going to do to get better? "I am looking at the brown target and pulling the trigger when I see my red dot flash. This is causing me to group very widely. I need to narrow my aiming point down to a coin-sized spot and I can shoot at the same pace with better hits." This statement is specific as to both the problem and the solution. The shooter will look to a small spot to fix the problem.

As you shoot, you want to build an understanding of the inputs coming from you and the outputs on the target. Again, do not be too oriented towards the result as far as target score and time. Try to build an understanding of how the gun is behaving in your hands so you can learn to make it do what you want.

Shoot the live drills in this book aggressively so you can learn how the gun is behaving and where you are falling short. You may find the drill times challenging, but when you try to meet them you will discover problems which, if you pay attention to and understand, you can easily solve using extensive dry training.

Once you are competent and safe, you need to give yourself permission to fail so you can learn to go fast.

TENSION

The topic of body tension bears discussion on its own. This isn't a specific technique element that you need to worry about. This is more a general bit of advice that you should pay attention to over the course of your training. If you are ever having problems progressing, you can often solve the issue by understanding that it may be caused by excess tension.

This is the key:

During your training, you should release all tension that is unnecessary or unproductive.

The first thing to understand is what productive tension is. For example, tensing up your support hand to get a good clamp on your rifle is productive tension. You are tensing up your muscles and expending effort but getting a return for it in terms of more stable behavior from your rifle during recoil.

If tension works its way into your firing hand instead of your support hand, you should expect to start pushing into the gun as you tense up and attempt to battle the recoil. Another thing that can happen is trigger freeze (not releasing the trigger enough to reset it to fire the next shot).

If you drive the gun around with control while you transition, that is good. If you become overtense in your shoulders and start to throw the gun from target to target, that excess tension will cause imprecision.

If a particular muscle tensing up isn't productive, you should try to let that muscle relax

so your body can work fluidly and naturally. The muscles you need to use when you are shooting are usually just your hands and arms. Allowing other muscles to tense up won't accomplish anything and will make multiple target engagements a lot tougher.

The idea is that you develop your skills and push yourself to go faster and faster. As you do this, you will find that your body tension changes. This is something you need to pay attention to. If tension works into unproductive muscles, it will cause problems.

First and foremost, pay attention to your hands. The most common place to have excess tension is in your firing hand. This causes trigger freeze and shanked shots, in addition to other problems.

The motion of your sights will tell you a lot; watching this will give you good information about your body tension. As you transition the gun from one target to the next, watch to see if your sights go past the intended point of aim and then return to the intended point of aim. This tendency to overdrive your target is usually driven by excess body tension.

Be mindful of your thought process and mindset while training. As you start to push yourself towards higher levels of speed and performance, you will see this change in mindset manifest itself in changes in tension. The more speed you ask of yourself, the more your body will tend to tense up. A very common event is having thoughts of going faster while the result consists of the shooter's shoulders, hands and entire upper body tensing up. The real trick is to keep pushing your speed and precision but minimize the excess body tension that creeps in, so you can stay relaxed.

Tension commonly changes as you pull the trigger. Be aware that your mind and body are going to react to the muzzle blast and recoil while fighting tension.

The bottom line is this: observe and understand how your body tenses up as you apply effort. Work to make your body cooperate. Pay attention, and you will improve.

MOUNT

How you hold your rifle will dictate how fast you can shoot it; this is the most important thing to understand when it comes to your mount. You can shoot slowly with a poor mount. When the speed ramps up, it becomes more and more difficult to maintain the pace with bad technique. You will eventually start to push or pull on the rifle as a reaction to the recoil, and your shooting will suffer. With a proper mount, you will be able to have the rifle be controllable and predictable in your hands.

As the drills you shoot become more complex, involve movement and multiple targets, etc., you will also understand the way the rest of your body can interfere with your mount if you don't train yourself properly. This book will ask you to push your shooting to the limit so you can really understand these things. You will learn to understand your tendencies and how to train to overcome them. Your self-awareness and the ability to understand and work through the material is key to putting this together.

The start position for most of the drills in this book is the hunt position (Figure 1). This position is where you are standing in an aggressive posture with your rifle sights held below your line of sight and a solid connection to the rifle established, with the safety on. If done properly, this position can only be maintained for a matter of seconds or short minutes before fatigue sets in. This position is utilized when you expect to use your rifle imminently. While moving, the connection to the rifle is relaxed in most cases.

Your mount needs to be consistent and durable. This means your mount should stay the same even after firing a few rounds. If it doesn't hold up to recoil without changing, then you have a problem.

Your mount needs to hold the gun stable and allow you to maintain mobility. It is imperative that you understand how all the parts of your body work together. Tension in one part of your body can cause tension in another. For example, tensing your back to try to control the gun will make target transitions a lot slower.

You should also consider how stock position interferes with body armor and equipment. Risers or stock cheek weld modifications may be needed due to any supporting gear you're

Figure 1: Example of the hunt position

using. This material was developed without risers and with a stock position that should work with or without armor. From that baseline, if you want to add a riser or move the stock position around, it shouldn't be a problem.

You want to wrap your support hand around the rail or forearm of your rifle with your thumb on top of the rail (Figure 2). It is important that you are consistent with your hand position so that you get consistent behavior from your rifle as it recoils. Using a reference point on your rifle to verify your support hand is placed correctly may be helpful. Examples are having a finger or thumb rest on top of or next to a front sight, pressure pad, mount for a light, etc.

Your support arm should put a very firm, neutral pressure straight back into your dominant shoulder. It is important that you pull the gun straight back in. If you try to pull on the rifle directionally to mitigate recoil, you will end up doing more harm than good for rapid-fire control.

Figure 2: Example of support hand placement

We recommend bending your support side elbow down and pointing it more toward the ground.

This will help keep the pressure straight back, especially under recoil. Very commonly, when shooters see their dot bouncing around, they start changing pressure with their support hand in order to get the gun to do what they want. Bending the elbow down keeps that pressure neutral instead of side to side. Side-to-side pressure on the gun is very difficult to do consistently. Hand pressure is the more complicated thing to take care of.

Your support arm is going to do the majority of the control of the rifle. We cannot emphasize enough how important that firm pressure is in order to get control over your gun. If you are shooting without a recoil-compensating muzzle device, you are really going to notice a difference with your support arm technique.

With your firing hand, you are going to hold the grip of your rifle. As long as you get high up into the grip, you should be in good shape in terms of positioning your hand. The more complicated thing to take care of is hand pressure. Hold the grip firmly with your firing hand, but no more than that. Pay careful attention to making sure you don't overtense or overgrip with your firing hand. This is going to slow down your shooting or possibly cause trigger freeze and induce you to push shots down low or left (for a right-handed shooter).

Conceptually, the best way to think about your mount is that you put all the pressure in with your support arm (Figure 3). You need to keep your gun in check. The rest of your

Figure 3: Key points of the mount

Figure 4: Example of head position

technique should be centered around holding the gun in place on your shoulder, not trying to control it. Your strong arm should keep the stock from shifting around, if possible. You are not trying to fight the recoil. This is a very similar concept to modern technique with a pistol. The support hand does the work, and the dominant hand does the trigger control.

Once you have your rifle mounted, you need to get your head position worked out. Bring your head down to the sights as much as you need to but try not to induce pressure onto the gun with your cheek (Figure 4). You want your cheek to stay in place, but you don't need to press into the gun.

The reason for this is that it is difficult to get all the different pressures of your contact

points to be consistent. You aren't going to have better control by using your cheek, but you can move the rifle around quite a bit.

The higher up your sight is mounted, the higher you can hold your head. It is more comfortable and natural to keep your head up and may actually be a requirement depending on your equipment. For example, consider if you needed to use a gas mask at the same time as your rifle. In contrast, having the sight mounted lower down will reduce the mechanical offset. This makes accuracy at close range a little bit easier.

In any event, try to get your equipment and head position sorted out so you are comfortable and consistent. Excessively pressing your face into the gun isn't helpful.

The best test for your mount is the Doubles drill. It is described in the advanced marksmanship section of this text. The gist of it is that you shoot rapid-fire pairs and assess the quality of your grip and body tension. You make sure you get your gun to behave consistently under recoil, so you can shoot it quickly and confidently.

Once you learn your mount in this fashion, we recommend doing a lot of dry training. This allows you to get the perfect mount of your rifle, so it is smooth and consistent for you to employ. Once you build the right habits in dryfire, the livefire should be much better.

STANCE

Having the proper stance is going to make your job of shooting much easier. More than that, how you stand influences how you move in and out of position and how well you can transition from one target to the next. It is important to understand that stance as a concept is more of a habit you strive to employ rather than something you can execute in a textbook fashion.

When you are moving around and shooting in a USPSA competition-style stage or similar dynamic shooting test, you are usually not in a textbook stance. It is important that you strive to consistently position yourself in the most advantageous way possible and that you continually review footage of yourself as you train and develop.

Ideally you should position yourself like a shortstop or a fighter (Figure 5). Set your feet wide apart and bend your knees. The idea is that you position yourself coiled up and ready to move out of position without requiring any redistribution of your weight or movement of your feet. This is a wider foot position than most people naturally want to shoot from, but it is advantageous. When your feet are set up in this way, you aren't inclined to pick a foot up and set it back down as you start moving out of position. Your feet are already wide enough.

It is helpful to bend your knees a fair bit. This helps you set yourself up into position more gently and allows you to shoot sooner. If you have knee or leg issues, it is also beneficial

Figure 5: Key points of the stance

because it reduces the strain on your muscles. You are setting yourself up to be ready to move.

You want to have a slightly forward weight distribution. Lean into the gun just enough to keep the muzzle down, but don't bias your weight so far forward that it puts you off balance. You don't want it to interfere with movement out of position as a result of needing to transfer your weight excessively when you start a movement. You will have a slight "lean into" the gun feel, and it will definitely help you keep your rifle in your shoulder pocket under recoil.

When you are shooting a rifle, it is helpful to drop your strong side foot back a bit, particularly if you are applying lots of pressure to shoulder the gun. Shooting with a more

41

square stance is also a good option, especially if you aren't using as much pressure with your support arm. This is based largely on shooter preference and equipment setup.

If you are shooting a gun with substantial recoil, you will do better shooting with the bladed stance. This would be something like 5.56 with an A2 flash hider muzzle device. This is especially true if the gun is very light with minimal attachments.

Bladed is not the preferred stance for shooting with a pistol. Being square to the targets is a better way to go. You don't have a stock that is going into a shoulder, so it makes the pistol much more neutral in terms of your body position. However, you should do just fine with a bladed stance. This is important when you consider transitioning from your rifle to your pistol.

When you transition to your pistol from your rifle, unless you are moving for some other reason, you usually don't want to move your feet as you do the transition. You really shouldn't move anything but your arms if you can help it. This will minimize the noise in your sights caused by your rifle bouncing around on the sling.

You should release unnecessary body tension, especially from your back and non-dominant shoulder. Having this tension will not help you transition the gun around any faster, but it will impact your precision. If you are constantly overdriving the gun during target transitions, carefully consider if excess body tension is the cause.

Unlock your knees and allow them to move as you transition the rifle around to various targets. This is different from how most people shoot handguns. It is helpful to use your knees due to the weight of the gun and the body position you need to adopt to shoulder the rifle. Be careful not to push the gun around too hard with your knees and cause imprecise target transitions. The only time you should really be pushing with your legs is when the target transition is very wide (something like 90 degrees).

Using the correct stance is a habit you do your best to build. When you are training shooting and moving at the range or at home, make sure you are setting up in the proper stance. Once you build the right habits, you won't need to think so carefully about them. Your stance can become an unconscious habit once the muscle memory is built.

Square Stance

If you prefer to eliminate the bladed posture of your feet, you can take a stance square to the target with your feet more parallel and get pretty much the same results (Figure 6). This technique is more neutral in many senses, and you can get a bit less pressure back into your shoulder. If you are shooting a low recoil setup, this may be the stance for you.

Figure 6: Example of the square stance

CONFIRMATION

onfirmation is one of the critical technical concepts in this book. This is the key to understanding how to break away from traditional marksmanship concepts and increase your speed.

Think about it like this: conventional firearms training really emphasizes the need to have sights aligned perfectly and have a very clean press of the trigger. If these two things happen, then the bullet is going to go right where it is supposed to.

Having your sights perfectly still on the target with a perfect sight picture, along with a very careful trigger press, will always get you the hits you want. The real problem is that this process is slow. If you want to learn how to go faster, the key thing you need to understand is that you are going to spend less time aiming in order to improve. You aren't going to "see faster." What happens is that you will learn to do more with less.

Another concept that needs to be understood is that of index or natural point of aim. What you will find with regular training is that you can generally look at a target you want to shoot and the gun will follow your vision right to that spot. People who train regularly are able to mount their gun on a target and have the sights show up more or less in alignment. This is why we use the word *confirmation* as opposed to aiming, because it is a closer reflection of reality. When you look

at a target and bring the gun there, generally you will see the sights and confirm the gun is indeed pointed where you thought it was. You normally don't fight to line up the sights. You just confirm what you think you already know and start shooting.

Aiming Schemes

As previously mentioned, a stopped and stable "perfect" sight picture with a very gentle trigger break is going to give you the highest possible level of accuracy (Figure 7). For that style of shooting, we prefer to focus on the trigger finger of our firing hand and press the trigger as carefully as possible. This style of shooting is only appropriate when the accuracy demands are extreme, due to the relatively large amount of time it takes to carefully press shots off.

When shooting at speed, you will not have time for slow and careful trigger presses.

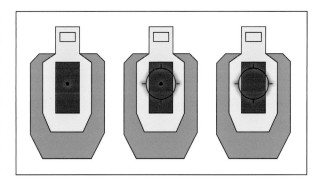

Figure 7: Example of stopped and stable "perfect" sight picture

You will need to rely on your ability to move your trigger finger quickly and independently without sympathetic movement from the rest of your hand. The ability to rapid fire without pushing the gun off target or attempting to fight recoil is something that most pistol shooters never really develop. It is without a doubt easier with a rifle, but it still isn't easy.

The next thing that gets compromised is shooting with the sights stopped and stable. As the speed picks up, you will perceive your red dot as a bouncing ball (Figure 8). Most people can shoot four or five shots a second pretty accurately. It takes a bit of training and understanding of how to interact with the gun, but it can be done.

As your shots start to speed up, we recommend you start reacting to the color of your sight rather than the sight alignment itself (Figure 9). As the targets get close and the speed potential increases, you should be reacting to seeing the color of your sight flash across the center of your intended target. This is a very quick confirmation and will give you lots of speed potential while still maintaining accuracy.

At very close range or in some awkward scenarios, you want to confirm the alignment of your gun just by seeing the outline of the gun itself superimposed over the target. If the range is close enough, this is all you need to confirm proper aim and you can start shooting.

These concepts can be understood in many different ways. For example, the system our friend Hwansik Kim created involves three "confirmations" for his red dot pistol shooting:

Confirmation 3: Stopped and stable dot on the target. Confirmation 2: React to the color of your dot on the target. Confirmation 1: Use the outline of your gun on the target.

This is a sensible and very easy-to-use system. It works quite well for its intended application.

For rifle shooting, things are quite a bit more complicated, but you can apply the same principles. You have windage/holdover issues at distance that cause problems. You also need to consider that the height over bore will affect where the bullets go at close range.

In long-range rifle shooting, many shooters use Christmas tree-style reticles with lots

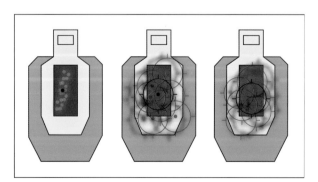

Figure 8: Example of red dot as a bouncing ball sight picture

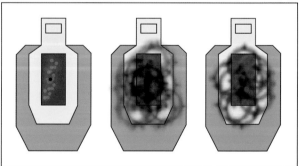

Figure 9: Example sight picture of reacting to the color of your sight

of hashes and dots that help them compensate for wind or bullet drop (Figure 10). The reason for all the extra marks in the scope is that it gives them a repeatable hold point they can calculate and thus use more informed holds. The thought process compared to using a plain duplex crosshair with which you would just guesstimate the hold is that if you aim at nothing, you will likely hit nothing. Knowing exactly where you need to hold to hit the target is very valuable.

One reticle we use is the 65/68 MOA ring with a small one- or two-minute dot in the center, used in the EOTech and Holosun optics (Figure 11). The reticle is very versatile and offers many aiming schemes. The large ring can be used to just center up a close-range target before firing, the small center dot can be used for shooting at distance or when precision is needed and the hash at the bottom of the main ring is calibrated to compensate for the offset at 7 yards (if the rifle is zeroed at 50/200 yards). All that having been said, we can also switch the Holosun reticle to a red dot only (Figure 12). We often just use it in that mode and compensate for the close-range offset with a holdover.

The best option for the style of shooting outlined in this book is to simply use a red dot and then memorize the correct aiming offset at each distance. At close range, you learn to look a bit higher up on the target than your intended point of impact. By the time the targets are 20 yards away or so, you can pretty much ignore the offset and look to the center of the target. On man-sized targets, you will get very good results doing this. When

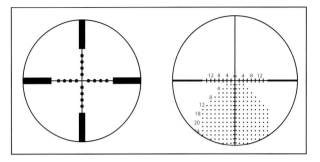

Figure 10: Example of long-range rifle shooting, Christmas tree-style reticles

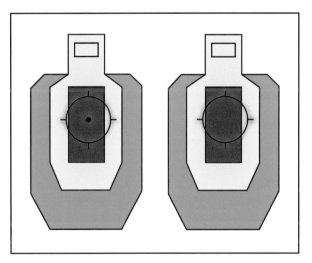

Figure 11: Example of EOTech and Holosun reticles

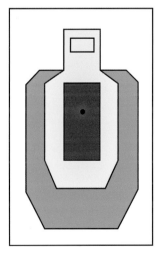

Figure 12: Example of red dot–only reticle option

things stretch to intermediate distances (60-100 yards) you will start needing to hold a bit low. This is important when shooting scorable paper targets or the small steel plates. Accuracy will really be tested.

If you have a lot of targets past 100 yards or target location is an issue, most people will prefer an LPVO setup. That isn't the up-close aggressive/practical style of shooting this book is built for. The drills in this book were developed with duty-style rifles, A2 flash hiders as muzzle devices and two-stage triggers. These are plain guns being shot really fast at close to intermediate ranges. Lots of distant targets isn't the concept behind this material.

As you train, we highly encourage you to experiment with using different aiming schemes. Do not think in terms of less or more, but rather reacting to the color of your red dot or making sure your reticle is stopped and stable before you press the trigger. Think about what you need to see from your sights as you visualize the drill. You will be shocked at what you can get away with after some training.

VISUAL FOCUS

Your vision tells your body what to do. If you think about it, you can understand that where you put your visual focus is where your attention will go. The more conscious you are about how you direct your attention, the better results you will get with any task. When it comes to shooting, the level of precision and how demanding you are with your vision will be reflected in your results. Deliberately looking at a small aiming area will get you better results.

Looking where you want to hit sounds easy, but there are all kinds of distractions that can happen. Sometimes competition shooters look at a tight partial target thinking "just don't hit that penalty target," while looking at the spot they are trying to avoid. Spoiler alert, the bullets will go where you look and if you are looking at something you do not want to hit, you will often hit it. Anyone who's ever participated in force-on-force training with airsoft or simunitions will likely say they have been shot in the hands. The reason is the shooter saw the gun and focused on that while shooting and their bullets just went where they were looking.

The more specific you can be with your eyes, the better the results will typically be. An example is looking at your target as a brown rectangular cardboard target, compared to looking for the A zone box. Better yet is trying to find the perforated letter "A" within the A zone of the target and staring a hole in the exact spot you want your bullets to go (Figure 13).

"Aim small, miss small" is a real thing. Another example is shooters looking at steel plates as one big plate or shape, instead of finding a crater near the center of the target and driving their vision to that spot. This is even more common if the steel is freshly painted a bright color.

When you want to insert a magazine into your rifle, you will likely get very different results if your vision is looking at the target as you bring a magazine up to the magwell, compared to looking down and watching the reload happen. To zoom in further, you will get the best result if you look at the magwell and bring the magazine to where you are looking, in contrast to looking at the round on the

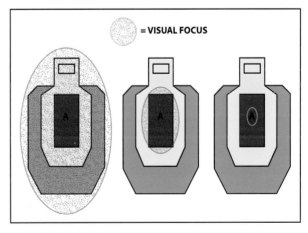

Figure 13: Examples of different levels of visual focus

top of the magazine as you try to guide it into the magwell.

Although it's a subtle change of watching the magazine move instead of looking at the magwell and bringing the magazine to where you are looking, the results will be quite different. Use that concept with respect to everything you do (Figure 14).

The last thing to be aware of is getting your vision pulled onto the sights/dot/reticle while shooting. Often the shooter wants to be sure of their sight alignment before firing, so they pull their vision back from the target to verify the sights are aligned, then just keep their focus on the sights as they continue shooting. You will lose precision and speed without realizing it if you are trying to locate your target while staring at your sights.

The best way to avoid any of the issues above is to mentally rehearse the scenario ahead of time, program where you want to look and what you need to see before you can fire. If you are training on a partial or hostage-style target, you should be deciding on an exact spot you want to hit before even starting the drill.

Occluding the Dot

As previously discussed, lots of bad things can happen when you have your vision in the wrong place and are not focused on the task at hand. Occluding the dot has been a very helpful tool to keep red dot shooters from staring at the dot when they should be staring at the target.

To occlude the dot, you just need to cover the front side of the optic with tape or a Kydex cover (Figure 15). While looking through the optic, you should be able to see the red dot clearly, but not be able to see through the glass. This can be used as a very helpful training tool to force you to stay target focused while shooting with both eyes open. If you shift your vision to the dot, you will see the covered window and it will be immediately obvious that you are looking somewhere you shouldn't be.

There are times you will want to remove the cover. Some of these are low ports, hard leans, or anything that will obstruct your vision and possibly only allow one eye to see the target. Occluding the dot is a great way to keep yourself honest about where your vision is focused. It is a great tool to use during dryfire practice as well as livefire, especially when working on target transitions. You will be shocked by what you learn about your vision when you train with an occluded dot.

VISUAL FOCUS
AT MAGWELL
FOR RELOAD

VISUAL FOCUS IS
NOT ON THE
TOP OF MAGAZINE

Figure 14: Example of visual focus on reloads

Figure 15: (L-R) 1: The dot can be occluded with tape, a cover, or even pasters. 2: Example of aiming with the dot not occluded. 3: Example of aiming with the dot occluded.

TARGET TRANSITIONS

If there is only one thing we can impress upon you regarding target transitions, it's that you will hit where you look. As mentioned in the section on visual focus, it's extremely important for you to look at the precise spot you want to hit. Through training, you can learn to program yourself to keep your focus on the areas where you want it to be.

Your Eyes Lead the Way

The timing of when you move your vision from spot to spot is also very critical. If you are sitting at your computer and you see the sale of a lifetime on something you want to purchase, your eyes look at the "Add to Cart" button, then your mouse cursor moves to the button and you click it. Imagine what would happen if you looked away from the "Add to Cart" button before your cursor got there. You could click the spot you meant to, be somewhat close, or miss it altogether.

The sights on your gun work the same way as a mouse cursor. You look at the spot you want to hit, you have the patience to wait until your sights get there, you fire, then after you fire the last shot on that target, you look for the next spot you want to hit. There is validity to the saying "aim small, miss small." The implication is that the smaller the area you are trying to hit, a miss just outside that area will still be in a tight pattern. The precision of your vision will affect where your bullets

land. If you look at the big brown cardboard target, your bullets will likely land in random places on the target. If you look at the very center of the target with intensity, you will have a much higher chance of hitting where you are looking.

Before even discussing aiming schemes and using the sights, we want to explain other ways your vision is essential and how important it is that you direct the order that you look at each task. Some of this may sound obvious, but think about it carefully compared to what you do when you are on the range.

The next thing to consider is wondering what your sights are doing while you are looking for a small spot on the target. It can be very tempting to shift your vision to watching the dot or reticle while shooting or transitioning between targets. The most effective way is to keep your eyes on the target once you find a spot you want to hit and bring the sights to where you are looking. After you are done shooting the target, your eyes should immediately look for the next target and let your sights follow. Your eyes always lead the way.

The physical part of how fast you can drive your rifle between targets is far less critical than most people think. Except for close-range shooting, the amount of control you have when moving your rifle between targets is more important than using all the muscle you have to push your rifle.

The ratio of speed versus control needed will change based on the size and distance of the target. The cost of using too much muscle to push the rifle is that it will stop imprecisely or require some time to wait for the sights to stop bouncing before you can fire. For situations in which the rifle has to travel a farther distance between targets, it works best to push the rifle for about half of the distance between the targets, then just let the sights glide into the target. Using your knees for wide transitions is very helpful so you can keep your upper body behind the rifle as you fire and avoid getting off balance. For very close target transitions, just look at the target with your eyes and let the rifle float to the point you are looking to. Pay attention to how the sights stop and assess how soon you could be shooting.

You Hit Where You Look

You hit where you look, for better or worse. If any part of the target draws your eye to it, then that's where the bullets tend to go. You need to get in control of what you are paying attention to and doing.

Remember that the target spot is not shape or color. You might see brown cardboard targets and hurry and just look to brown. You will likely hit brown, just not in the center of the targets. The same thing happens on painted steel targets. People tend to just look for the color and shoot at that, instead of driving their vision to a small spot in the center of the steel plate.

Control

Go as fast as you can with control. We often tell students to work at the speed of their vision. Don't try to push the gun around; look exactly where you want the sights to go and let the gun arrive there. It is generally counterproductive to push the gun from target to target.

Focus on having your sights arrive on target, stable and ready to shoot. The ability to look at a spot and have the sights arrive there in a direct line without any extra movement or corrections needed is what you should strive for. This is the mark of an advanced shooter. They don't tense up and throw the gun around. To a spectator, it will often look uneventful since the shooter is in complete control.

Only once you have really developed your transitions should you worry about swinging the gun around. Drills like Wide Transitions will teach you a lot about unlocking your knees and driving the rifle with precision.

RELOADING

Reloading your rifle is not a skill that is usually emphasized. There seems to be a belief that it isn't a very important skill because actually needing to do it in a real-world scenario is unlikely. This is a sensible way of thinking from that perspective. However, there are still good reasons to learn to nail fast reloads (for example, clearing malfunctions rapidly should they occur).

Reloads are not complicated. You just eject the previous magazine and get a new one into the rifle. Accomplishing this smoothly and reliably is what you should aim for. A blazing-fast reload that looks good on social media is not necessarily required, but you should aim to at least be proficient. When you decide to reload your rifle, you should be able to get it done consistently, if not fast.

Initiate the reload with your trigger finger while going for the spare magazine with your support hand (Figure 16). The most important thing during this phase is that you try to hold the rifle still. The more stability you have, the better. This will make everything easier during the rest of the process. The inability to hold the rifle still while trying to guide the magazine to the rifle is one of the main issues we see with students' reloading technique, so pay attention to it.

We recommend grabbing the magazine with your support hand in a "beer can" grip (Figure 17). Wrap your support hand around the magazine with your thumb behind the primers for your cartridges. That hold gives the best control.

You might notice that it is difficult to get a "beer can" grip when using a closed-top pouch or a chest rig. The fastest reloads are going to be done from open-topped belt pouches. As of this writing, there doesn't appear to be a faster way to do it that is practical enough to actually wear. We recommend you place a single open-topped magazine pouch on your belt, then have a more secure storage solution for additional magazines (Figure 18).

If you wish to have the means to retain spent or partially spent magazines, a dump pouch on your belt is a good way to go. It's nice to segregate the used magazines from the fresh ones, and the dump pouch does that well.

Make sure you get the magazine seated all the way. Lots of shooters will unnecessarily tap the magazine repeatedly after it's inserted into the rifle. A helpful tip from Matt is to consider the angle at which you are applying pressure while seating the magazine (Figure 19). The extra force applied at an angle will not work as well as just pressing the magazine straight into the magazine well. It is helpful to look the magazine into the gun and keep your eyes on the magwell until the magazine is in. Once the magazine is inserted, you should shift your eyes to the next task.

Figure 16: Example of initiating the reload with the trigger finger while going for the spare magazine with the support hand

Figure 17: Example of "beer can" grip

Figure 18: Example of a single open-topped magazine pouch

If you need to release the bolt before you can fire again, you should look at the bolt catch. If you are using a B.A.D. Lever or other bolt assist device, shift your vision to the target right after you see the magazine inserted into the rifle. It is important that you don't have your eyes still looking at the rifle when you should already be shooting. If you are confirming the sight picture on the target sooner, it will get you shooting a lot sooner.

After you manage the bolt catch (if needed), you need to get your support hand back onto the rifle. This is another area with a big potential for mistakes. You want to develop a nice

Figure 19: Example of proper angle of the magazine for reload

Figure 20: (L-R) Example of mounted vs. underarm assault reloads.

consistent remount of the rifle so you can get back to shooting. Developing a consistent position for your support hand to return to is critical. Suggestions for building a reference point are resting your thumb against, behind or on a pressure pad, flashlight housing or mount, laser, or front sight. You need some feeling or reference point to make sure you are contacting a repeatable point with your support hand.

Another consideration is that you have a choice for where you hold the rifle when you reload. The main question here is whether you should pull the stock off your shoulder while you reload or not. If you take the stock off your shoulder, you can drop the gun down a little bit. Some people actually prefer that. If you can keep the stock fixed to your shoulder, it will keep the rifle much more stable.

Matt differentiates these two as "mounted reloads" and "underarm assault reloads" (Figure 20). Situation and personal preference will determine which style you use. For standing reloads, keeping the rifle mounted to your shoulder will give the fastest results. It's easier to keep the rifle stable, and you can easily look at the magwell to guide the new magazine in. This does require more arm strength than dismounting the rifle, but it is faster when done properly.

If you are moving or are in a compromised shooting position, you will have better luck with the underarm assault reloading position. As you are ejecting the magazine, the rifle should be dismounted, and the buttstock should be under your armpit while being pressed into your side. After you have the new magazine seated, remount the rifle as you would normally.

PISTOL BASICS

Pistol shooting is not the focus of this book, but it is something that you need to be proficient with in order to pass the CQB Warmup.

You need to be able to draw and fire six rounds into the A zone of a USPSA target set 10 yards away in under 2.5 seconds. If you can do that, you will be fine to tackle all the content in this book.

Make sure you grip your pistol high up into the beavertail with your dominant hand (Figure 21). We recommend pulling the trigger by using the first joint of your trigger finger (if possible) to get more leverage on the trigger. This is platform-specific, but we strive to do it with all of them. The added leverage makes guns like Glocks with long trigger travel or heavier triggers much easier to deal with.

You should only grip your handgun with your hands and forearms. You do not need to use your back or chest to hold the gun and it will likely cause issues if you do. Your firing hand should hold the gun with just enough pressure to ensure that it doesn't move around inside your hand while shooting. You shouldn't have a sensation that your firing hand is fighting the recoil.

It is helpful if your support hand does the majority of the gripping force and control on your pistol (Figure 22). You should have a sensation that the pistol is locked into your support hand. You don't need to grip your firing hand fingers - you need to grip the pistol itself.

Figure 21: Key points of grip on the pistol

Figure 22: Key point for support hand on pistol grip

It is not important that you are high up on the gun - it is important that you grab as much of the surface area of the grip as possible. This is lower down on the gun. The gun should feel like it is locked into your support hand.

During fast shooting, you should feel like the gun doesn't slip in your hand at all.

It is counterproductive to try to stop the muzzle of your pistol from rising. Instead, look at the spot on the target you want the gun to return to and let it return there predictably. You shouldn't feel like you are fighting to hold your pistol down. Fighting with your pistol usually leads to a bunch of low hits.

Shoot the advanced marksmanship drill Doubles with your handgun from 5, 7, 10, and 15 yards to make sure your grip is solid and that you are focused on the center of the target. If your hits are concentric, but widely dispersed, you aren't target focused. Lots of low and left hits indicate a right-handed shooter fighting with the gun and pushing the gun with their firing hand or forearm (Figure 23). Doubles will help you understand what a correct grip feels like.

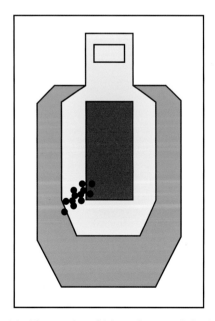

Figure 23: Example of hits when a right-handed shooter is fighting with the gun

Once you understand your grip, strive to draw to it quickly and repeatedly. Often when training with a pistol, the draw to first shot time is emphasized over every other factor. You will grow more as a shooter working to draw to a secure and reliable grip as quickly as possible. This will sacrifice one or two tenths of a second, but in the end your shooting will be much, much better. If need be, you can always rip a fast draw with a marginal grip and fire a super quick first shot; it just shouldn't be the emphasis of your training.

Dryfire with Your Pistol

A very important drill you can do with your pistol is Trigger Control at Speed. To do this drill, you aim your unloaded pistol at a target and set your timer for a random delay. At the beep, press your trigger back on your pistol immediately. The idea is to fire the shot within 0.25 seconds or so of hearing the beep (you should be done pressing the trigger before the end of the start signal). Do not "prep" your trigger for this drill. All the trigger pressing must be done after the start signal. This will force you to move your trigger finger quickly. It will also help you assess sympathetic movement from other muscles in your hands. Strive to move your trigger finger independently so you can press the trigger immediately without the sights moving. You should also do the drill with your trigger finger in different starting locations. This will help you react to the beep in different scenarios, such as resting on the trigger, just out of contact with the trigger, and having your trigger finger outside the trigger guard.

Train yourself to draw your pistol up to a sight picture very quickly. Eight-tenths of a second to draw, get a perfect grip and get your pistol aimed at a 7-yard target is pretty good. If you can do that out of a retention holster in one second, you are doing quite well. It's important not to press the trigger while you are doing this drill. Instead, only assess how the sights stop on the target, the placement of your hands on the gun, and the pressures you are applying.

Another important thing to practice is transitioning from your rifle to your pistol. You can mirror your static draw time transitioning from your rifle. Make sure your support hand guides the rifle down to your side and then gets over to your pistol. Your feet should stay as still as possible so that you don't disrupt any of the mechanics of slinging the rifle and drawing your pistol.

The dryfire you do with your pistol is going to be seriously beneficial in terms of both your pistol shooting and your rifle shooting. You should work to master a solid grip and good trigger control with your pistol. If you are interested in going further with that, there are plenty of other reading materials you can reference listed at the end of this book.

PISTOL TRANSITIONS

Pistol shooting is not the focus of this text; however, there is definitely a need for discussion of transitioning from rifle to pistol. This is a core skill if you are training as a martial art and wish to be able to use a long gun and a sidearm together.

Before we get into the specifics of transitioning from rifle to pistol, there are some safety issues to discuss as well as some practical realities.

You are going to be swapping out your live rifle for your live pistol. If you get hurt doing any of the techniques discussed in this book, it will almost certainly be related to your transition/draw technique. Most accidental discharges are going to happen around these techniques, so it is important to be extremely careful as you train yourself. You want to build good and productive habits so you can start going fast and still be safe.

That having been said, a big area of discussion around transition technique will be the safety on your rifle. Conventionally, when you put a gun down or reholster it, you are going to want to apply the relevant safeties in order to make sure you don't have an accidental discharge. This is logical and important.

When transitioning from your rifle to your pistol at speed, you will find that applying your safety to your rifle at speed is very challenging. Getting the safety positively engaged

and then initiating the transition to your pistol is going to chew up some time.

At this point, it's good to discuss the practical reality of actually transitioning to your pistol from your rifle. If you are engaging a target with your rifle and the trigger goes dead (maybe you are out of ammo, maybe there is a malfunction) you can either choose to fix the problem with your rifle or switch to your pistol. When actually doing this under practical circumstances, the safety issues are mitigated quite a bit. To put it a bit more bluntly, why would you insist on applying the safety to a rifle that is out of ammunition as you switch to your pistol? It doesn't make sense in a practical setting.

The training setting is a lot different. If you are training transitioning to pistol and you're dropping your rifle without putting it on safe, you need to worry about catching the trigger on some piece of equipment and sending a round off. Having this happen with someone standing next to you could obviously be a disaster. Your own foot might get hit in such an instance. It is seriously dangerous to be transitioning from a loaded rifle to a handgun without using the safety.

One way around this is to set your rifle up so that when you transition to your pistol, your rifle is actually empty. That is a viable and safe way to train rifle to pistol transitions.

During your dryfire training, attempt to safety the rifle as you transition to your pistol. This means that you make a good faith attempt to get the rifle on safe every time you transition to your pistol at speed. This extra layer can help protect you from an accident during your live training.

The bottom line is that this is an area where there is serious potential for an accident, but there are also real-world reasons you may choose not to use the safety when you transition from your rifle to pistol. Be very careful to train yourself to be safe, and don't build habits that are going to injure you or someone else.

The only transition this book will have you do (during the last drill of the book, CQB Warmup) is with an empty rifle. Once again, if you choose to train transitions, train to be careful.

With all the safety stuff out of the way, a good goal is to have your pistol-to-rifle transitions look very similar to simply drawing your pistol. The goal here is to have minimal disruption or "noise" in your technique. You don't want to be in the habit of throwing your rifle down to your side as you grab your pistol. You want a nice clean draw of your pistol while you place your rifle down at your side on the sling.

Starting from your rifle mounted and pointed at the target, you should use your support hand to guide the rifle down to your side as gently as possible (Figure 24). This will need to be done quickly of course, but in the end, you want your rifle down at your side with minimum swinging around or destabilization. You should resist the urge to just drop the gun and go for your pistol. You really don't want to be battling your rifle swinging around while you are trying to use your pistol.

When it comes to your firing hand, as soon as you have dealt with the safety on your

Figure 24: (L-R) 1: Rifle mounted and pointed at a target. 2: Apply safety or confirm out of ammo with the firing hand. 3: Use the support hand to guide the rifle, while the firing hand goes to draw the handgun.

Figure 25: (L-R) 1: Once the rifle is on the side, release the support hand. 2: Draw pistol and bring the support hand to pistol. 3: Establish grip and shoot.

rifle, you should be going for your handgun as normal. There is nothing that changes from your conventional draw. Get your hand to your gun.

When you have a firing grip on your pistol, it's time to release your support hand off the rifle and let it hang. From this point on, it is a conventional draw stroke.

Draw your pistol as normal and get a solid two-handed grip.

Once again, the key element here is to minimize noise in your movements. Extraneous or violent movement will disrupt your shooting and you don't want that. Instead, look for a fast and fluid transition that doesn't look too different from simply drawing your pistol.

FAQ

Where should I get targets to train with?

- You can purchase cardboard USPSA targets online at a number of stores. Typically purchasing them in boxes of 100 is the best value when you figure in shipping charges.

Should I just mark my hits with a Sharpie as opposed to covering the bullet holes with masking tape or target pasters?

- It's very important to be able to tell where all the bullets are going. Targets get very tough to read if you are only marking with Sharpies, and you need to be able to tell exactly where the bullets hit for each series of runs. Using masking tape or target pasters is highly recommended to patch holes.

How often should I patch the targets?

- We recommend doing three to five repetitions on a drill before patching the targets. Before you patch the targets, examine them and look for big

picture trends or themes from which you can draw conclusions about your shooting.

How do I decide which shot timer I should purchase?

- There are a lot of options and features, but there are three features we value the most. First, the menu needs to be easy to navigate so you can change between using a par time and adjusting the delay of the beep after pressing the start button. Second, having the ability to adjust the volume of the beep is very nice if you dryfire indoors or have others around you while you're dryfiring that might not appreciate a loud beep. Lastly, you want a model you can easily change the battery in. Purchasing something rechargeable prevents you from getting it back into service quickly, without waiting for it to charge.

What is the "hunt" position?

- The hunt position is starting with the stock connected to your shoulder with the safety on and the optic just below your line of sight.

How hot should I let my rifle and handgun get?

- Handguns rarely get so hot you need to let them cool off. Rifles can get too hot after just a few magazines of rapid fire. Overheating your rifle can cause accelerated wear. If the rifle gets so hot you can feel it through the handguard, you are risking damage to continue rapid fire. If you can, try to switch back and forth between multiple rifles during training. Take advantage of cooling time to do the drills in dryfire.

If I take a few weeks off training, how much will it hurt my performance, and how long will it take me to get back to where I was?

- You will be surprised how fast things come back. In most cases, within a few dryfire sessions you will feel back up to speed and ready to start improving.

What should I do if I have a bad range day where nothing seems to go right, or I'm just not feeling it?

- Don't burn through ammo if you don't feel like you're being productive. Sometimes adding some perspective is very helpful. Try taking a few steps back and thinking about the big picture. Asking yourself what is occurring in your training is better than just shooting more.

I feel that my gear is limiting my progress, but I do not have the available funds to purchase new gear. Do you have any advice?

- Train with what you have and you might be surprised by what you can accomplish. If you are convinced that your gear isn't good enough, it won't be good enough. Instead, work to do the most you can with what you have. Your attitude will determine a lot.

I feel like I am constantly messing up in dryfire, and I am making mistakes over and over.

- If you are happy with all of your dryfire runs, you are fundamentally doing it wrong. You should train yourself to be conscious of everything that happens and that will make you more effective at fixing it.

How much ammo do I need to get really good?

- There is far too much emphasis placed on how much time or resources are needed to reach your goals. Those things are important, but there are lots of shooters that have fired tens of thousands of rounds and never had noteworthy improvement. You can get scary good with a few thousand rounds of ammo, a shot timer and a very strict assessment of your daily dryfire training.

How often should I dryfire?

- Everyone has different levels of availability but doing focused dryfire for 15-20 minutes a day for four or five days a week will yield excellent results. The frequency of your dryfire practice is far more important than having one large weekly dryfire session. Training daily or every other day will keep you very familiar and sharp.

What is predictive shooting?

- Predictive shooting means aiming once and pulling the trigger twice. You will be shooting at a speed where you can't see each sight picture before you fire, but training and experience will allow you to predict where the shots will likely go.

What is reactive shooting?

- Reactive shooting means you see each sight picture before you fire the shot, but you don't overconfirm and stare at a sight picture like you would for bullseye shooting. It's typically used for precision shooting or shooting more difficult shots at a practical pace.

What is hit factor scoring?

- Hit factor scoring is calculated by taking the points earned and dividing it by the amount of time it took. Example: 51 points ÷ 5.06 seconds = 10.07 hit factor.
- The points system can vary based on discipline, but the system we use is: Alpha = 5 points, Charlie = 2 points, Delta = 1 point

DRILLS

BASIC MARKSMANSHIP

This section dealing with basic marksmanship and safety should accomplish a few things for you, especially if you are brand new to shooting. You need to walk before you can run. This section is designed to do that for you.

You will zero your rifle and do some slow-fire group shooting. This ensures that the gun hits where you point it, and that you know how to operate it. There are exercises that will help you learn your offset. The height over bore causes problems, especially at close range. It is imperative that you are able to hit different targets at different distances without any time pressure before you start trying to go fast.

Similarly, you should practice indexing (pointing) your rifle and reloading your rifle from a belt pouch. This should be done slowly without ammo before you attempt to do it quickly. The 10-yard Bill Drill also deserves an explanation. The drill will teach you to shoot fast and control your rifle by establishing a firm connection to it.

When you are comfortable with the basic marksmanship section, we recommend you shoot the CQB Warmup Basic Standard and decide where to go with your training based on your assessment from that drill.

Safe Handling

Balancing speed and accuracy will always be a sliding scale as you improve at shooting. Safety is nonnegotiable. Become familiar with how your rifle operates so you can load, unload, fire, and maintain muzzle control without any supervision.

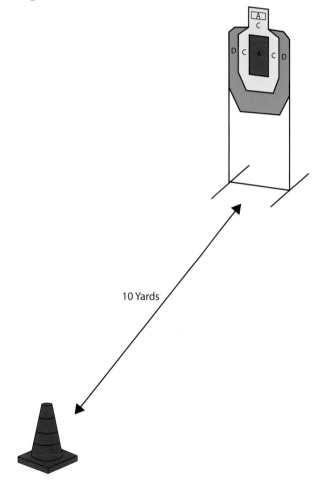

10 Yards

Procedure:

Start in the hunt position with the safety on. Upon the start signal, fire two rounds into the target, reload the rifle, and fire two more rounds for a total of four rounds fired.

Assessment:

No time limit. All actions should happen sub-consciously without pausing to think about what needs to happen next.

Corrections:

This drill will teach you the value of dry-fire. Simply learn to handle your rifle reliably and effectively.

Tips:

Look at what you are doing. Shift your vision from target to magwell, to bolt release, and back to the target.

Dryfire Workup:

Practice dryfire mounts and reloads.

We recommend getting dummy rounds you can use in your magazines so you can practice mag changes with a realistic weight. Using ammunition made with no powder and no primer works just fine.

Groups

The ability to send bullets exactly where you want them to go is the most important part of shooting. Before adding in the time components, it's imperative that you are able to shoot your rifle accurately. This skill will be built upon in later sections.

Procedure:

Shoot the smallest five-shot group possible while standing unsupported.

Assessment:

Acceptable: As and close Cs
Good: all As
Possible: shot group under 1"

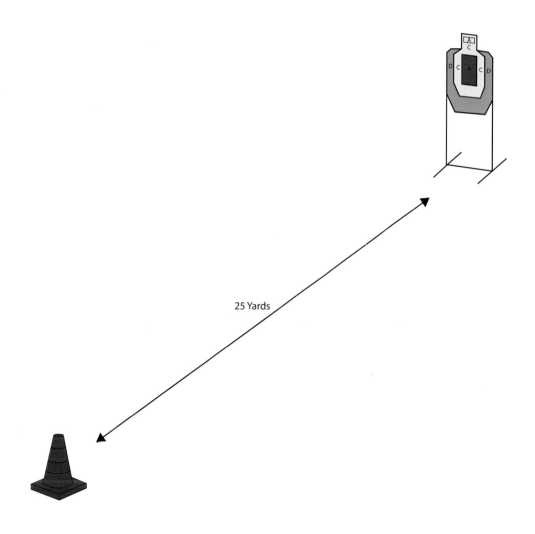

25 Yards

Corrections:

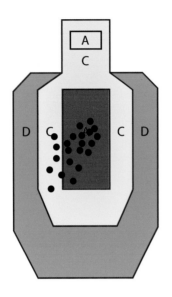

Low and left hits are a result of pushing into the rifle while firing the shot.

Tips:

Place more focus on your firing hand pressing the trigger rather than focusing on trying to hold the rifle perfectly still.

Dryfire Workup:

Pick a very small spot on the target and press the trigger slowly to drop the hammer without moving the sights. Start with using a braced position (such as prone), then progress to standing and dryfiring the rifle while unsupported.

Once the sights are on target, you should place your primary focus on your grip and pressing the trigger straight without influencing the rifle.

Ready Up–10 yards

This drill is the equivalent to doing a draw with a handgun and it's just as difficult. Train yourself to stare a hole into the target and bring your sights to where you are looking. Be mindful of using too much tension or muscle, as it will result in your sights stopping inconsistently on the target.

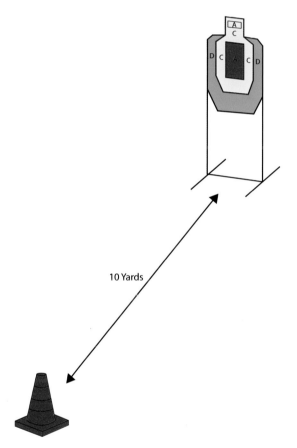

10 Yards

Corrections:

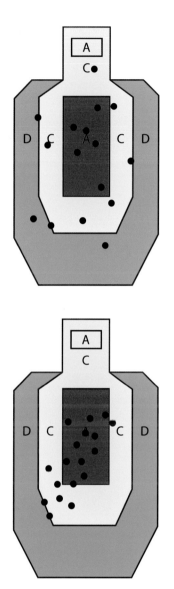

Procedure:

Start in the hunt position with the safety on. Upon the start signal, fire two rounds into the A zone of the target.

Assessment:

Acceptable: 1.0 second
Good: 0.80 seconds
Possible: under 0.60 seconds

Inconsistent hits are usually due to inconsistent mounting of the rifle. The rifle needs to behave the same way every time when bringing it up to the target and applying pressure to control the recoil. As you increase speed, this will become difficult to do consistently.

A seat belt pattern on the target will likely be due to a combination of an inconsistent mount and pushing into the rifle while firing.

Tips:

Look to a small spot above the center of the target. Be aware of how your sights move when you bring the rifle up. As you go faster, you will likely overpush the rifle. You want it to come to a gentle stop right where you are looking. Your sight movement will tell you everything.

Live ammo will reveal if your mount is acceptable or not. Make sure your dryfire includes training yourself to use the appropriate pressure to control live ammo.

Strive to shoot much tighter than just the scoring rings of the A zone. At 10 yards the rifle should be very compliant for you.

Dryfire Workup:

Have the rifle on safe in the hunt position. Make sure your eyes are looking at the target before the timer goes off. On the start signal, bring the sights to where you are looking while deactivating the safety, without pressing the trigger. Use a 0.40 par time.

Assess your success by how well you are able to bring the sights to where you are looking on the target and the manner in which the sights stop. Make sure you don't throw the rifle up into the target. If you don't carefully bring the gun up, you will be imprecise.

Make sure you have a very firm mount during your dryfire. You need to train good habits.

Josh's GCW (Gold Calculator Watch) Drill

This drill introduces aiming schemes and mechanical offset from height over bore. Changing from a coarse aiming scheme to a very refined sight picture is often used in dynamic shooting. It can be very difficult to program yourself to change gears and aiming schemes, so visualizing the drill before you attempt each repetition is a good habit to start.

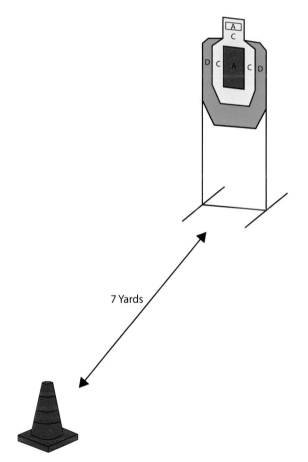

7 Yards

Procedure:

Start in the hunt position with the safety on. Upon the start signal, fire two rounds into the lower A zone, two rounds into the upper A zone, then two more rounds back into the lower A zone for a total of six rounds fired.

Assessment:

Acceptable: 3.0 seconds, all As
Good: 2.2 seconds, all As
Possible: under 1.5 seconds, all As

Corrections:

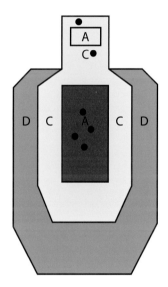

Sporadic hits on the upper A zone are typically from not changing from the aiming scheme used on the lower A zone. Make sure you recover the sights for the second shot in the head box (reactive shooting).

If your hits are grouped in the wrong place, make sure you are looking at the precise spot you want to hit, and are using the correct hold to accommodate for height over bore. You will need to look for a coin-sized spot at the top of the head box in order to hit the upper A zone.

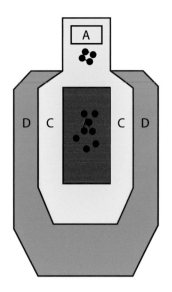

Tips:

Make sure you are changing aiming schemes between reacting to the color of your reticle to seeing a stopped and stable sight picture.

Dryfire Workup:

Do the drill dry and work faster than your desired livefire goal time. Make sure you transition the rifle precisely from point to point. Make sure you press the trigger firmly for each dryfire shot. Your goal is to identify trigger control issues as well as transition issues.

Bill Drill – 10 yards

Shooting the rifle straight without pushing into it while maintaining a proper grip is a lifelong pursuit for many shooters. Pay close attention to the grip you use with each hand and observe how the sights move differently if you adjust your grip while shooting. Train yourself to keep the exact same grip for the entire drill.

Procedure:

Start in the hunt position with the safety on. Upon the start signal, engage the target with six rounds.

Assessment:

Acceptable: 1.8 seconds, all As
Good: 1.5 seconds, all As (hits in a small group)
Possible: under 1.1 seconds, all As

Corrections:

If you experience trigger freeze, make sure you are relaxing your firing hand.

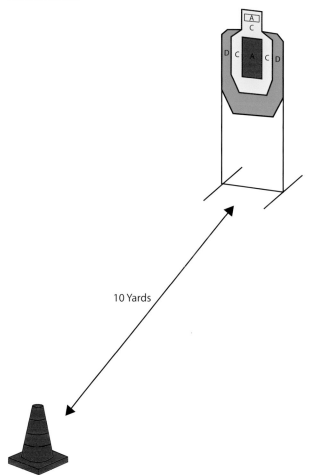

10 Yards

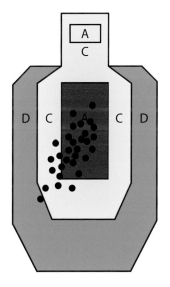

Low and left hits will likely come from pushing into the rifle while you are firing it. Make sure you don't add additional pressure onto the rifle in the middle of the string.

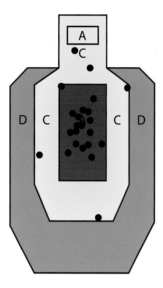

Random hits are likely caused by not holding the rifle into your shoulder firmly. Visual imprecision is another cause. Wait for the dot to flash in the center of the target.

Tips:

Look at the exact spot you want to hit before the timer goes off, then bring the sights to where you are looking. You will want to have a firm connection to your rifle established in your shoulder pocket as you await the start signal. This will help you be more consistent.

You will probably have an easier time learning if you develop your 10-yard Bill Drill to a high level before you start working at longer distances. You can assess your mount and connection to the rifle pretty easily at close range. You will have an easier time restoring your target and get your training done sooner if you don't have far to walk. The relatively easy marksmanship challenge at 10 yards will really help you be aggressive on the trigger. Pay attention to how your sights track in recoil and assess your mount for durability, consistency, and predictability. Once you understand how your gun will behave in your hands and are gripping it properly, you can really attack the other drills. This is very easily accomplished at 10 yards.

Dryfire Workup:

The most important thing to work on for the 10-yard Bill Drill is your consistent mount of the rifle. Try a simulated 25-yard target in your dryfire space. Start with the rifle shouldered, but in the hunt position. Your goal is to be able to start from the hunt position and get a sight picture on your target with the rifle firmly mounted. Safely and accurately aim the rifle and deactivate the safety in about 0.60 seconds.

ADVANCED MARKSMANSHIP

Once you understand basic safety and marksmanship considerations, you should step into the advanced marksmanship drills. These drills are critical for you to understand both the mount as well as your capabilities. The mount can be summarized as your connection with the rifle. As your ability to mount the rifle improves, so will your ability to shoot the rifle accurately at fast speeds.

This section will likely be the most difficult to master. The drills here will set you apart from other shooters if you are able to stack bullets on demand. You will likely consume the most ammo on these drills compared to all other areas of your training. This is normal and good. If you master your mount in the context of these drills, it will help all other aspects of your shooting.

To further relay the importance of this section, consider this:

The first year Ben shot the Doubles drill, he shot half the ammo he consumed for that entire year on that one handgun drill. That's 50,000 rounds on a single drill in a calendar year. That number should explain the importance of mastering shooting Doubles.

Practical Accuracy

This is the ultimate test of reactive shooting. The goal is learning how to stack shots on top of each other by pressing the trigger straight with a sense of urgency, without fighting or pushing into the rifle.

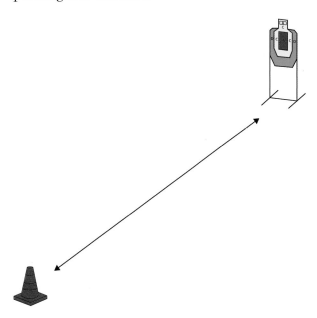

Procedure:

Start in the hunt position with the safety on. Upon the start signal, engage a small spot in the center of the A zone with six rounds. Fire follow-up shots as soon as your sights recover. There is not a specific time limit, but the idea for the exercise is to shoot as soon as the sights recover.

This drill replicates the type of shooting appropriate for a tighter shot or a distant target where you need to have accuracy without slowing down to bullseye speed.

For reference, reactive shooting is in the 0.20- to 0.35- second range typically. You shoot when you perceive your dot has returned to the aimpoint from recoil. If you sit on and stabilize the dot, then carefully press the trigger, you aren't doing the drill correctly. The idea here is to learn to shoot at the pace of your vision.

Assessment:

Acceptable: A zone hits at 20 yards doing 0.30 splits.

Good: A zone hits at 25 yards doing 0.25 splits.

Possible: A zone hits at 50 yards doing 0.25 splits or faster (muzzle devices and triggers affect this quite a lot)

Corrections:

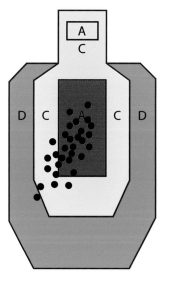

Low and left hits are almost always caused by pushing into the rifle as a way of trying to fight or stop the recoil while shooting.

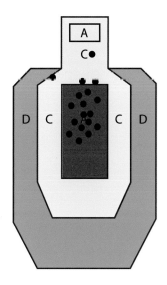

High hits generally come from insufficient support hand pressure or from shifting your vision onto the sights themselves instead of the target.

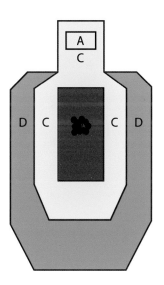

Even if your target looks great, back up or go faster. You won't learn much by repeating what you already know.

Tips:

Pay close attention to the feel of your gun in your hands. Once you feel yourself making a mistake with your grip or trigger control, you are going to be able to correct it easier.

Look at the spot on the target you want to hit. Do not look for the target's outline or at the color of the target. Look at a very specific point.

Dryfire Workup:

Trigger Control at Speed is a great drill for learning to press the trigger fast without pushing into the rifle. The drill is very simple. Start with your rifle aimed at a target and set your timer for a random delay beep with a minimum time of over two seconds. Press the trigger the instant you hear the beep without making the dot move at all. You should be done pressing the trigger before the end of the start signal.

There are a few ways to cheat the drill that you should avoid at all costs. First, you must maintain a proper mount of the rifle, including the grip pressures you would use if you were firing live ammo. Holding the rifle loosely will make for good results in dryfire that will not translate to livefire. Second, backing off on the speed component of reacting to the beep or pressing the trigger slower or more deliberately will make it much easier to produce results that look good. This is equivalent to "slowing down and getting your hits" and will not make you improve.

As you work on the drill, experiment with different starting positions with your trigger finger. As you move your finger farther away from the trigger, the drill will get more difficult. Start from contacting the trigger, to having your finger barely off the trigger, to starting with your finger towards the front of the trigger guard.

Doubles

This is the ultimate way to learn your mount. By pushing the limits in terms of your speed and distance, you will learn to manage the rifle by adjusting your inputs and examining the effects.

This drill will get you results. There is a lot to be learned about what different inputs you impose onto the rifle and how important consistent grip pressure is. You will learn to shoot as fast as you can, pull the trigger and control your rifle in a predictable and repeatable fashion.

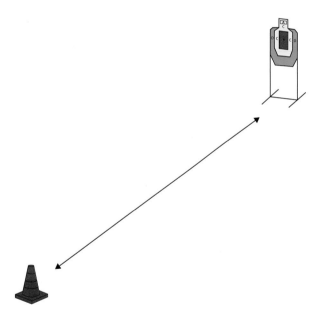

Please note that this is a very foundational drill. This is classified as an advanced marksmanship drill because doing the drill correctly is not easy. No matter what level shooter you are, you should always push this drill to where you start failing. In doing so, you will learn some important lessons. Paying attention to the right things will save time, ammo, and frustration.

Procedure:

Start in the hunt position with the safety on. Upon the start signal, get your proper grip and aim the rifle at the target. Engage the target with four pairs of shots. Each pair should be fired as fast as you can pull the trigger. Allow the gun to completely quiet down from recoil before firing the next pair. Return your trigger finger to a relaxed position between pairs of shots and take all the time you need to return the sights to the center of the target between pairs. There should be an audible pause between pairs.

Repeat this procedure for multiple strings. Shoot this drill at any desired distance.

At closer ranges, you will shoot extremely aggressively and can use the drill to get acclimated to the recoil. Try truly shooting as fast as you can pull the trigger inside of 10 yards.

You can fire an aggressive pair of shots that both strike the target as far as 50 yards or further. There is no reason to limit yourself before you even start experimenting.

Make certain you look at a coin-sized spot in the center of the target and try to drive each bullet to that spot. Even though you will be shooting fast, keep your eyes open and observe your sight movement. Adjust your technique (inputs) to get stable and consistent behavior from your rifle.

The idea is to shoot your rifle (within the bounds of safety) in such a way in order to learn what you can and cannot get away with when firing rapidly. You should learn how your rifle reacts to your inputs. Competitive shooters will frequently shoot this drill with more than 10,000 rounds a year.

This is also a great test for the effects of equipment changes such as springs, muzzle devices, trigger changes, etc. Equipment can be tested in the rapid-fire setting much more efficiently than in slow fire.

Assessment:

Acceptable: 0.20 or less splits into the A zone at 10 yards

Good: 0.20 or less splits into the A zone at 15 yards (shooter is able to "call" shots and articulate the effect of inputs on the rifle)

Possible: 0.20 splits into the A zone at 25 yards or further (with competition muzzle devices and triggers the distance can extend quite far)

Corrections:

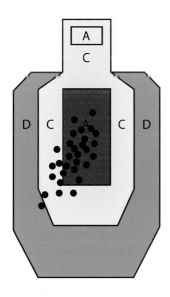

Hits trending low and left will likely be due to pushing into the rifle while firing as a way of fighting the recoil. It is common to throw your dominant shoulder into the stock of the gun or to pull the gun down with your support hand.

If the sight is moving more than you think it should, pull the rifle tighter to your shoulder with your support hand.

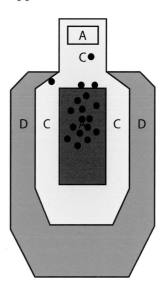

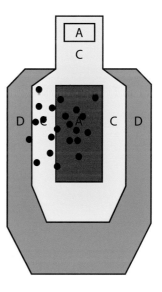

High hits generally come from insufficient support-side pressure or from shifting your vision onto the sights themselves instead of the target. If you get sucked into the dot, expect to see this happen.

Pushing into the rifle with your shoulder as you attempt to fight or reduce the recoil will push bullets to the left.

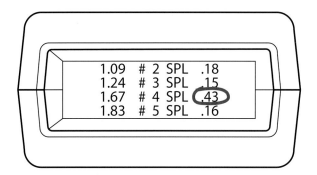

Trigger freeze can occur due to an overly tense firing hand not relaxing enough to reset the trigger between shots.

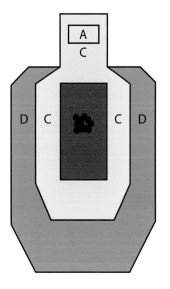

You should always be assessing if you could have done better. Were you pulling the trigger aggressively or as fast as you could? Were you aiming for each shot fired when you should have been shooting predictively?

Tips:

Try this drill at different yardages from 5 yards all the way out to 80 yards (or more). Observe what is actually happening as you shoot. Don't be too focused on the result; focus on how and why the result came about.

Dryfire Workup:

To work up for Doubles, you simply do the drill in dryfire. Try to recreate trigger control issues that you are experiencing with live ammo.

Press the trigger aggressively, then take your finger all the way out of contact with the trigger. Smash the trigger back in order to simulate hand tension that comes from live ammo being fired. Once you can simulate the issue, you can work through it.

Bill Drill – 50 Yards

Stretching Bill Drills to 50 yards is an excellent way to develop and test your shooting.

Procedure:

Start in the hunt position with the safety on. Upon the start signal, engage the target with six rounds.

Assessment:

Acceptable: 6.0 seconds, all As and Cs
Good: 4.0 seconds, all As and Cs
Possible: under 3.0 seconds, all As

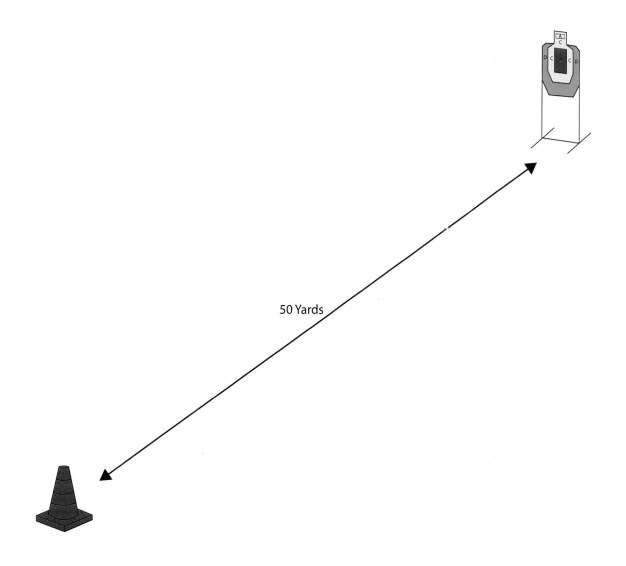

50 Yards

Corrections:

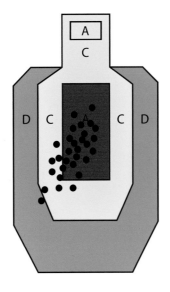

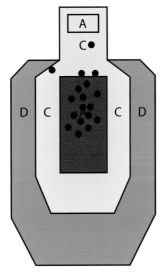

Low and left hits will likely come from pushing into the rifle while you are firing it.

High hits generally come from insufficient support hand pressure or from shifting your vision onto the sights themselves instead of the target. At 50 yards, it is more common to start chasing the sights visually.

Pulling your rifle into your shoulder harder with your support hand is very critical on this drill.

Tips:

There is an amount of patience required to wait until the sights are centered back on the target. It is very common for shooters to pull the handguard sideways with their support hand to get the dot to return faster. This is usually a subconscious microadjustment, not a deliberate choice. This sort of thing tends to snowball over the course of shooting the drill. Once you start torquing the rifle around, it tends to get worse.

Experiment with dot brightness to determine if you have a preference. Oftentimes, a shooter will start staring at the dot if the brightness is turned way up.

Dryfire Workup:

The main thing you need to consider here is the speed and consistency of your mount. For dry training, we recommend training to index the gun on a simulated 50-yard target. You could go further with that if you want to. The bottom line is that you should practice getting your rifle pointed at the target, getting the safety off and having your sights stable on said target in one second.

Variations:

It's smart to work your way out to 50 yards instead of starting at 50 yards from the beginning. If you are looking to crush at distance, work your way back in 5- or 10-yard increments. Start with fast Bill Drills at 10 yards (under 1.3 or 1.4 seconds) and start adding distance incrementally. Things will slow down as you work your way back (obviously), but you will learn control much faster by shooting really aggressively.

Many people are inclined to start very accuracy focused, then work towards going faster. You will not truly understand the proper connection to the rifle without shooting extremely fast at closer yard lines.

Mad Max's Diagnostic Drill

Understanding how various inputs affect how the rifle tracks is important. Yes, you need to pull the rifle with your support hand; however, depending on how your rifle is set up, you may need to do a bit more or less work. Duty-style rifles with flash hiders will require more work than rifles with adjustable gas systems and compensators. Every rifle behaves a bit differently. This is a good test to do when you are trying to determine the correct grip and pressures needed to keep the sights tracking back to your aiming point. This drill came from Max Latulippe.

Shoulder/aim the rifle at a small spot on your target. Do not add more inputs than just holding the gun naturally. Fire one round and do not bring the sights back to the point of aim after recoil. Just let it stop wherever it goes and then fire a second shot. Pay close attention to the direction the rifle recoiled and how the sights tracked as well as the visual reference for how far away the second shot is from the original shot. Try each of the following steps while using the same two-shot process and work towards mounting the rifle in a way that it returns to exactly where you are aiming.

- Add support-side pressure, fire again at your original aimpoint and observe how the sights track.
- If shots are still to the right, add a bit of strong-side shoulder roll.
- Adjust (add more roll) until the gun returns to the original point of aim from recoil (windage only).
- Too much shoulder roll will push the sights to the left after recoil (for a right-handed shooter).
- Play with different pressures for elevation.
- If your forearm is too high above the barrel (tactical shoulder shrug over the barrel), the dot will return lower than the original point of aim.
- If your forearm is too low without support-side pressure, the gun will recoil higher and stop higher than the original point of aim.
- If you hold the forearm low/parallel with added pressure into the strong shoulder it should recoil straight back to the original point of aim.

Once you find the proper inputs for the specific gun/load you are shooting, you can now rip Doubles and troubleshoot yourself as you go.

TARGET TRANSITIONS

Target transitions are one of the most mis- understood concepts of shooting. Remove any preconceived notions of "driving the gun" or muscular strength being relevant to the task. Instead, place an extremely high level of importance into where you place your vision and the amount of tension you carry.

Confirmation Drill will help you under- stand the minimum-needed sight confirma- tion to make any given shot. You don't usually need to see your red dot or reticle stopped and stable. In many cases you will be surprised by what is possible when you bend the rules of conventional marksmanship.

Blake Drill is a good basic target transi- tion drill. The real challenge is that everything happens so fast and small mistakes lead to very big errors.

Rifle Cross will make sure that you under- stand offset. The credit card shots are very challenging to hit at high speeds. The sequenc- ing and switching between aiming schemes and the engagement order in itself is a very difficult challenge and a good test of your mental rehearsal and visualization before you attempt the drill.

Accelerator will help you change aiming schemes (confirmation) on the fly. You should attempt to break conventional marksmanship rules and push to the point of failure as you learn what rules can be broken, and which demand respect.

Wide Transitions will show you how to let your lower body get involved as you transition your rifle around. Unlock your knees and let the rifle glide between the targets. Learn the importance of getting your vision ahead of your sights as you seek out the center of each target as you battle tension.

Confirmation Drill

"Don't criticize mistakes; analyze them."
                    —Hwansik Kim

Our very dear friend Hwansik Kim created this drill and it's often misunderstood. Do not attempt to master this drill. However, you should be paying very close attention to the results various inputs yield and you should be thinking about how you can apply them to your shooting.

Procedure:

Start in the hunt position with the safety on. Upon the start signal, engage the target with one round using the indicated confirmation level below. Repeat each confirmation level for five repetitions, then assess the results and think about how they would apply to different targets. Please see the tips section for more information.

Confirmation 1:

Kinesthetic alignment only. You "feel" your arms are pointed in the correct place and then you shoot. No visual confirmation.

Confirmation 2:

You react to the color of your sights crossing your intended aiming area. With an optic, you shoot as soon as you see the optic color or crosshair, which means you will just see your dot streak across the target. With an iron sight setup, you shoot when you see the color of your front sight.

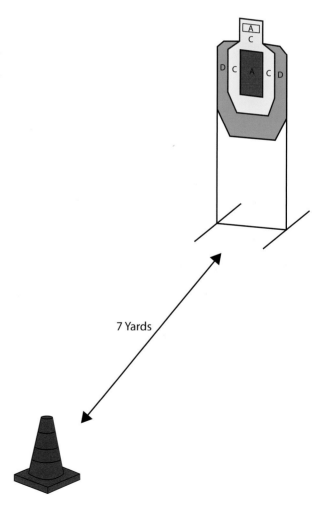

7 Yards

Confirmation 2.5:

You react to the shape of your dot or reticle in the aiming area. Your dot looks like a dot but is still moving. This is what happens frequently on mid-range targets. If you shoot with strong control, your dot will be stabilized as it comes into your aiming area.

Confirmation 3:

Your dot or crosshair is stopped and stable in your intended aiming area. Your dot should appear as a dot and not as a streak. With iron sights you should see the front sight stopped through the rear sight. This type of aiming scheme consists of a near-perfect sight picture.

As you move up in confirmation levels it will take more time, but the result on the targets will be much cleaner.

Shooting iron sights, you might find it useful to distinguish between a perfectly aligned sight picture and seeing the front sight through the rear sight, but perhaps a bit misaligned. You might think of the sights slightly misaligned as another Confirmation 2.5.

Corrections:

It's important to understand that this drill is designed to be a learning exercise only. There is no limit to what you can experiment with on this drill. Just remember, your goal with the drill is to put in a specific aiming scheme and then assess your outcome. You are not trying to get a good or bad outcome. You just want to see how it all works. Once you get a sense of this, it should be easy to apply these concepts to the rest of your training.

Tips:

This drill was developed by Hwansik Kim to isolate the effect of the aiming strategy, confirmation level and aiming scheme on the target.

The component of target acquisition and engagement - where you have a lot of control over speed - is how you aim the gun at the target. More specifically, it is the reference you are using to confirm the gun is aimed. Traditionally, the expectation is that every sight picture looks the same on every target. People are generally trained in nonpractical shooting contexts to get a perfect sight picture for each and every shot, but that is not the expectation here.

Learning how much of a "perfect" sight picture you can trade away to go faster is one of the most important things that a practical shooter can do. As soon as you understand what sort of sight picture will produce what sort of outcome, all you need to do is train yourself to address each target with the optimal strategy and your results will be excellent.

This exercise exists to strip away every other layer and show you the effect of the aiming strategy on the target outcome.

Dryfire Workup:

Be sure to do this drill dry and pay close attention to what you see just at the moment you press the trigger. You want to be very skeptical of Confirmation 1 being done in a dryfire setting. You don't get visual confirmation of anything, and it is very easy to train bad habits. Save Confirmation 1 for the shooting range only and in a very limited context of testing it.

Blake Drill

Target transitions are a very important skill, and this drill will be a big test of your vision. Not waiting until the sights get to the center of the target due to lack of visual patience, or not finding the center of the target with your eyes, will result in very sporadic results.

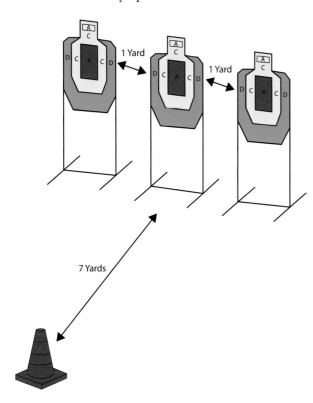

Procedure:

Start in the hunt position with the safety on. Upon the start signal, fire two rounds into each target.

Assessment:

Acceptable: 2.0 seconds, 4 As and 2 Cs
Good: 1.6 seconds, 5 As and 1 C
Possible: under 1.4 seconds, all As

Corrections:

Drag-on or drag-off hits are typically related to vision. Make sure you are looking at the spot you want to hit, and you are keeping your eyes on the target until you are done shooting it.

Drag-off occurs when you look away from the target before you are done shooting it.

Drag-on occurs from firing before the sights arrive at the point you want to hit.

Tips:

Remember the importance of looking at the spot you want to hit and letting your eyes drive the rifle, rather than forcing the rifle to move with your body.

Dryfire Workup:

Do the drill without pressing the trigger while using a par time. Focus on precise stops on each target, especially in the middle. Do this to train your eyes to look at that spot on the target you want to hit. It is very easy to start following your dot on this drill, which is what you want to avoid. Omitting the trigger press will make your assessment much easier.

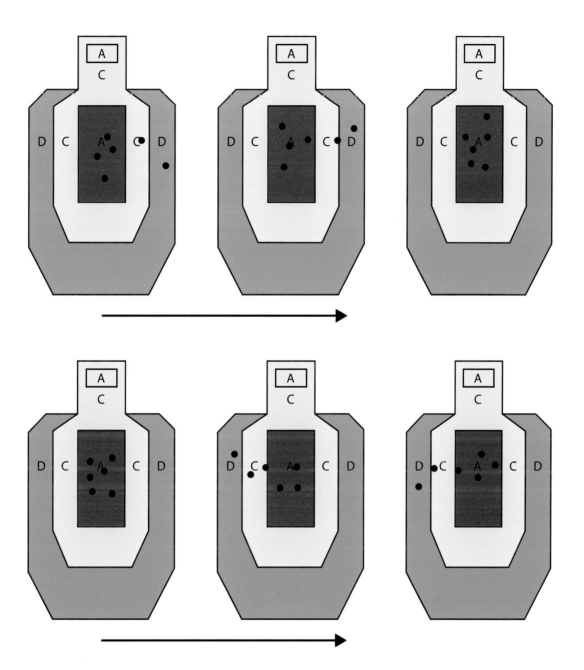

Rifle Cross

This is the ultimate test for precise target transitions while changing aiming schemes, height over bore offset and confirmation levels. Dryfire repetitions before firing any ammo is highly encouraged. Place all your mental focus on using the correct aiming scheme for the given target as you rehearse the target engagement order.

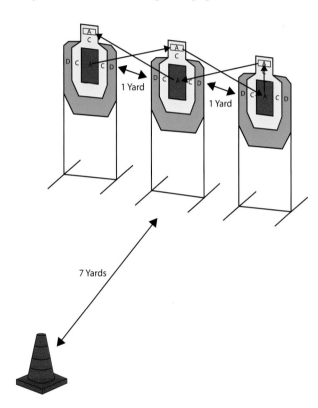

Procedure:
Start in the hunt position with the safety on. Upon the start signal, engage the upper and lower A zones in a crisscross pattern from left to right with two rounds each; on the end target, engage the second A zone with two rounds, then work back across, engaging the remaining A zones with two rounds each. At the end of the drill, you should have engaged each body and each head, firing a total of 12 rounds.

Assessment:
Acceptable: 6.0 seconds, only As and Cs (less than half Cs)
Good: 5.0 seconds, only As and Cs (less than 3 Cs)
Possible: under 4.0 seconds, all As

Corrections:
Sporadic hits on the upper A zones are likely from not changing aiming schemes after engaging the lower A zones. Make sure you have a stopped stable reticle before pressing the trigger.

Tight groups just below the upper A zones are usually caused by not using the correct holdover for your optic offset.

Pairs on the target that are close together but in the wrong spot are likely caused by not looking at the exact spot you want to hit. In most cases you need to look substantially above the point of intended impact in order to account for the offset.

Tips:
Be mindful of the power of your vision. Make sure you are looking where you need the sights to go and confirming you are seeing the correct sight picture for the target difficulty before firing. Once again, look where you need your sights to go. When you understand your offset, this will make sense.

If you really enforce Confirmation 2.5 shooting on the head boxes, you will get a lot more Alpha hits up there. For example, shoot your red dot like a bouncing ball rather than a predictive hammer and you will likely get better hits.

If you want to try a fun variation of this drill, add a mag change after you shoot the

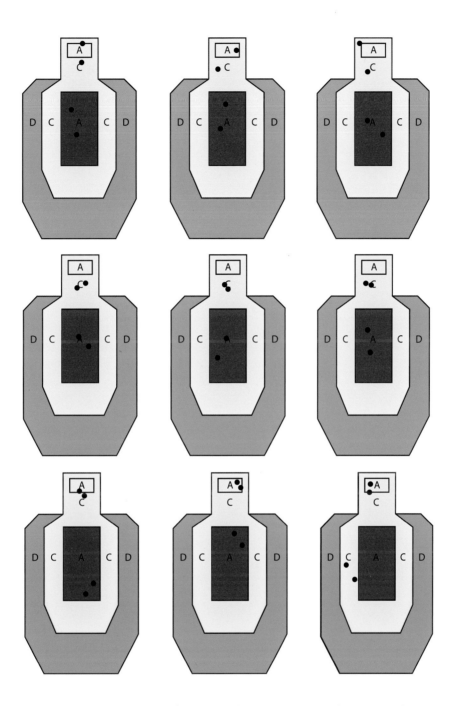

third A zone. Pay close attention to make sure your mount doesn't change from before to after the reload.

Dryfire Workup:

Mentally rehearse the engagement order so you can move from target to target without hesitation. Emphasize a clean precise stop on the upper A zones and make sure the sights come to a full stop.

Program in the correct color confirmation on the lower A zones. You should be firing as soon as you see the color of your reticle in the A zone.

Accelerator

This is one of our favorite drills and will likely be something you revisit throughout your training. This drill tests your ability to change aiming schemes and confirmation levels. The detail of the visualization before attempting each repetition will likely correlate to the result. It is also recommended to experiment with aiming schemes. Often, you might be surprised by what you can get away with.

Procedure:

Start in the hunt position with the safety on. Upon the start signal, engage each target with two rounds.

Assessment:

Acceptable: 4.0 seconds, 2 Cs
Good: 3.0 seconds, 1 C
Possible: under 2.5 seconds, all As

Corrections:

If you are getting sporadic hits, consider refining your aiming scheme.

The middle target presents the most difficulty for most people. Make sure you are stopping the gun on the target while you shoot it, as opposed to sweeping through without stopping the sights. Pick a small spot on the center target with your eyes. Keep your eyes there until both shots are complete.

Tips:

The big lesson on Accelerator is that you should think in terms of process and not pace.

Look at the targets in terms of efficiency of the aiming scheme that you are going to apply, not in terms of how fast you go on each target. This will make a big difference to your outcome. Thinking "speed up" or "slow down" is a lot different than thinking "stop my vision in the center of the target."

Practice shooting the targets from near to far and far to near. Training in both directions will reveal your weaknesses. This is how you are going to grow as a shooter.

Make sure that you apply different aiming schemes to the targets. On the back target, you are probably going to need to fire a pair of shots using reactive shooting. The dot will take a bit of time to come back down and you will need to be patient.

It is very common to have your dot brightness too high and for it to cause problems at this distance. If you focus on the target, the dot will return without much effort. If you chase the dot visually, the shooting becomes much more difficult.

On the mid- and close-range targets, you can get away with shooting pairs predictively. If you have a problem with accuracy, you likely have a problem with your connection/mount consistency with the rifle. Another big possibility is that you are not looking for a small spot on the target. If you just look at brown on a USPSA target, you will likely hit brown - but not necessarily the A zone.

Dryfire Workup:

You could train a rough approximation of this drill on dryfire targets. Commonly available

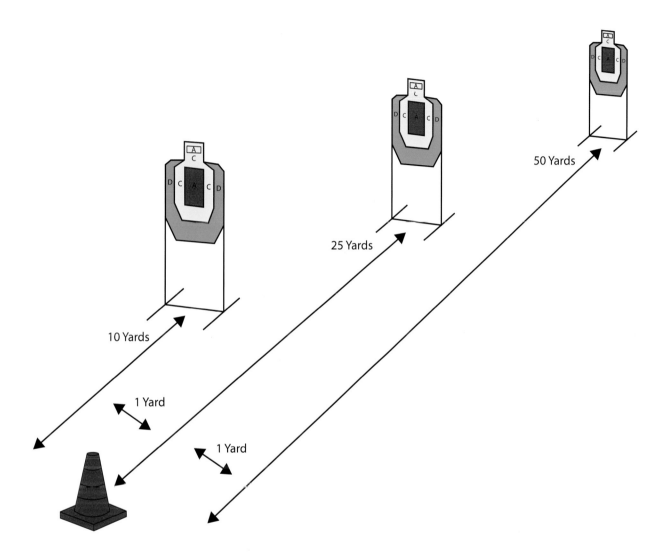

sizes are ½ scale, ⅓ scale, and ⅙ scale. That would be a pretty good setup to train this drill at home.

The major thing that is hard to train doing at-home dryfire is the focal depth changes between the targets.

There is a difference between targets all set on the same wall in your dryfire area and targets that are actually set at different distances. Your eyes need to adjust between the targets if they are truly at different distances. If you have some way to actually set the targets at different distances in your dryfire area, you should do that. Otherwise, make sure to do dryfire on the livefire setup of this drill to get your eyes used to it.

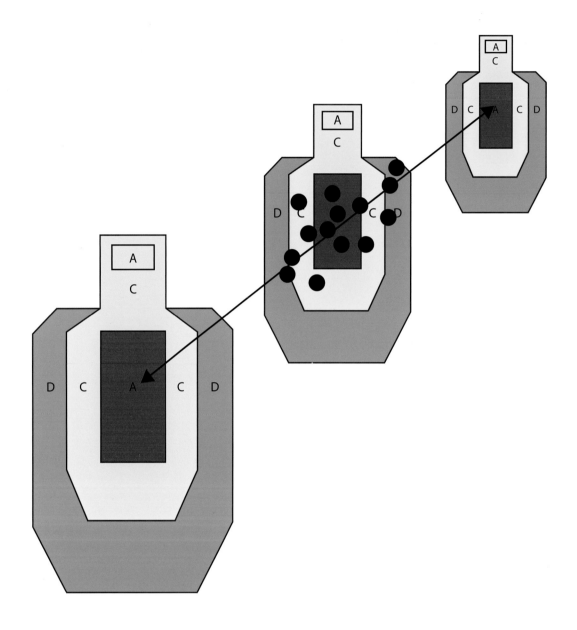

Wide Transitions

Wide transitions are a lot tougher than they look. Important things to remember are setting up wide and remembering to look where you want to hit. For wide target transitions, you will need to use your muscles and unlock your knees to push the rifle to some extent. You will need to experiment to learn what will work best for you. Pushing the rifle half of the distance to the target, then letting it subsequently float into the target works pretty well for most.

Procedure:

Start in the hunt position with the safety on. Upon the start signal, engage the middle target, then engage the left or right target, then the center target again, followed by the remaining target you have not engaged, then engage the middle target a third time for a total of 10 rounds fired. An example order is middle, left, middle, right, middle.

Assessment:

Acceptable: 5.0 seconds, all As and Cs (3 Cs maximum)
Good: under 4.5 seconds, all As and Cs (2 Cs maximum)
Possible: under 4.0 seconds, all As.

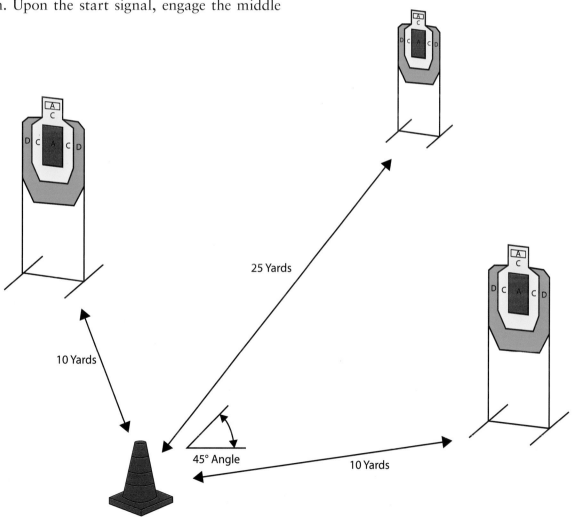

Corrections:

Tight groups that are in the wrong place on the left and right targets are likely caused by not looking at the center of the target. Make sure you look at the exact spot you want to hit.

Drag-on or drag-off hits are typically related to vision. Make sure you are looking at the spot you want to hit, and you are keeping your eyes on the target until you are done shooting it.

Drag-off occurs when you look away from the target before you are done shooting it.

Drag-on occurs from firing before your sights arrive at the point you want to hit.

Pushing the rifle too hard will cause it to overswing the target, sending shots to the outside edge. The correction is to make sure you aren't pushing on the rifle more than a third to a half of the distance you are transitioning, and looking at the exact spot you want to hit.

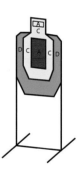

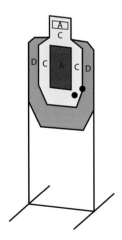

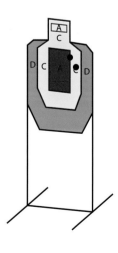

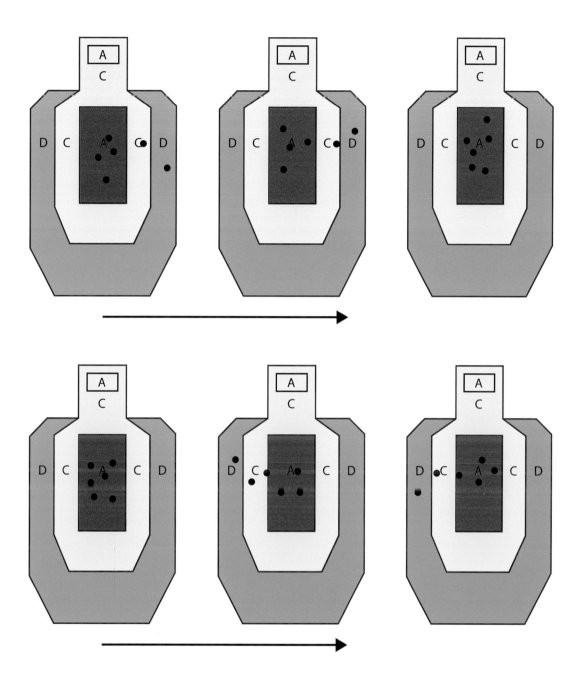

Tips:

Experiment with how much muscle you need to use to move the rifle on the wide transitions. Pushing the rifle roughly half of the distance between the targets then letting the sights glide into the target will typically give the best results.

You need to allow your head to come off the gun as you transition. This drill is set up with wide transitions to encourage this as much as possible. This will help you get used to leading the gun with your eyes and allowing your head to move freely when needed.

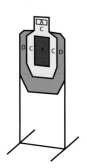

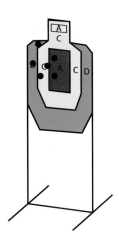

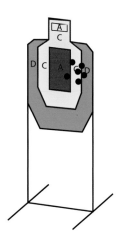

Dryfire Workup:

It is easy to practice for this drill using a corner in your house, provided you have a safe backstop. You can place targets on each wall of a 90-degree corner in a room and get used to transitioning back and forth to prepare for this exercise.

Variations:

Consider working a very wide transition. Shoot the middle target first and last. The other six rounds go into the left or right target, transitioning every two rounds. The order would be middle, left, right, left, middle or middle, right, left, right, middle. This is a fun variation if you want to make things really tough.

MOVEMENT AND POSITIONING

The movement and positioning drills are designed to help you get used to the idea of shooting and moving safely and efficiently. There are a few elements to pay attention to and we will discuss all of them. The drills will teach you the concepts when you do them.

Pay attention to safety as you start running around. If you have safety angle considerations at your range, you should plan your movements accordingly. It is difficult to observe a "180-degree" safe angle when you start running around with rifles on slings. Make sure you are within your range rules and be smart with your shooting when you get into movement and livefire.

We recommend that you put the rifle on safe if you are going to dismount it to run. This is a good practice to get into and is required of most of the military and law enforcement officers that shoot practical rifles in a work setting.

Bar Hop and *Track the A Zone* are both drills that are designed to get you shooting as you are destabilized. They will emphasize how important it is to disconnect your upper body from your lower body while shooting on the move.

Go Stop and *Positionator* are going to help you shoot as you move into a position from a run. They will keep you honest with respect to your footwork and test your ability to move in and out of a shooting position aggressively, but efficiently.

All in all, these are a very good set of drills to work with.

Bar Hop

This drill teaches you to shoot when the sights tell you to, rather than when your feet are in a specific placement. Learn to disconnect your upper body from your lower body: your upper body doing the shooting while your lower body carries you across the stick. You should begin and end the drill in your normal shooting stance with your feet spread apart and your knees bent.

Procedure:

Start in the hunt position with the safety on. Upon the start signal, fire two rounds into each target while standing on one side of a stick or board, then step across the stick or board and fire two more rounds into each target while standing on the opposite side from where you started. Make sure your stance is correct when you start and finish the drill. You will fire eight rounds in total.

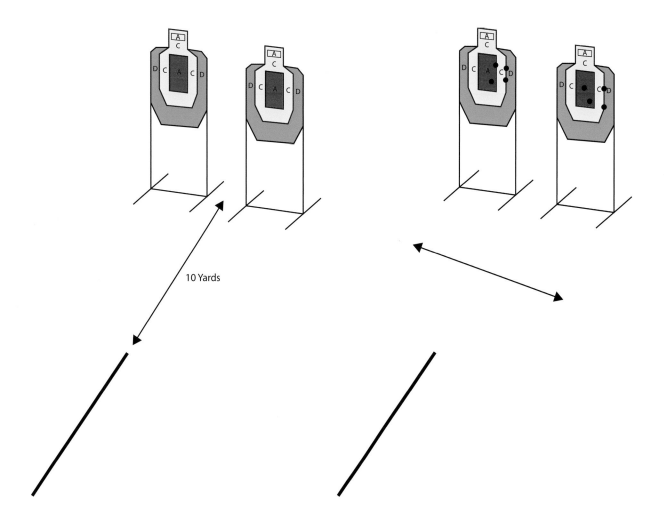

10 Yards

Assessment:

Acceptable: under 3.0 seconds, all As

Good: 2.5 seconds, all As

Possible: under 2.2 seconds, all As

Corrections:

Be mindful of what your vision is focused on. Switching your focus to the reticle, front sight, or dot will likely force you to drag hits in the direction you are moving. It is imperative that you focus your vision on the center of each target as you shoot it - your sights should be blurry.

Make sure you finish the drill with a nice aggressive shooting posture. Your feet should be spread apart, and you should be ready to move. This is a very difficult element to incorporate into the drill because you will not be punished on the timer or with the hits if you don't follow this rule.

Tips:

This drill is a bit of a brain twister. Do dry repetitions until you can remember the engagement order without hesitation and get your feet to cooperate with you.

Don't place a large focus on watching for foot faults while doing the drill. The stick is just to force you to move while you shoot. The big takeaway should be learning to disconnect the shooting while your feet carry you to the next position.

Dryfire Workup:

The footwork element of this drill needs to be mastered in dryfire before attempting this exercise with live ammunition, especially if you are paying for your own ammo. The footwork is challenging.

Track the A Zone

This drill (developed by Hwansik Kim) teaches you how to "track" the A zone efficiently. The movement and vision barriers are used to make visually tracking the target spot much more difficult.

Procedure:

Engage all the targets in the sequence of your choosing. It can be any order. 1 2 3 4, 4 3 2 1, 2 1 3 4, etc. The only consideration is about where the targets are shot from. You always shoot target 1 from the left side of the

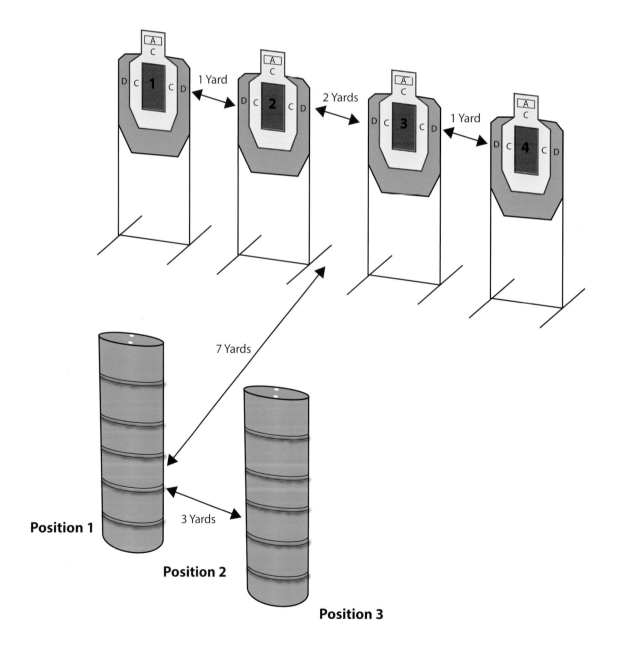

vision barrier (position 1). You always shoot target 4 from the right side of the right vision barrier (position 3). Targets 2 and 3 are shot from the zone in between the vision barriers (position 2).

It is not a requirement of this drill that you be forced into any leaning. Do not place down fault lines.

Assessment:

Acceptable: 4.0 seconds or less, all As and Cs
Good: 3.5 seconds, all As and Cs (maximum of 1 C)
Possible: under 3.0 seconds, all As

Corrections:

If you focus on your front sight, dot, or cross-hair instead of a small spot on the target, expect

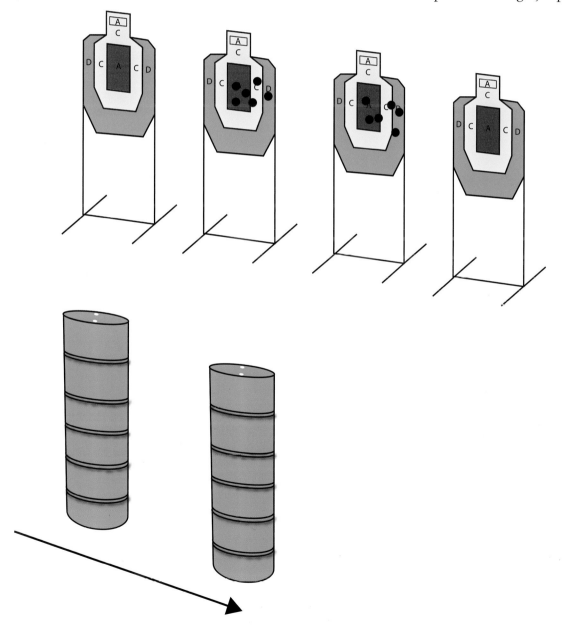

to see hits dispersing in the same direction you are moving. Return to target-focused shooting to correct this issue. Your sights should be blurry.

Hits on the outside edge of the last target you engage is usually due to shooting when you see your sights touch the target.

It is very common, especially as people speed up, that excess tension in the upper body builds up and the transitions between targets become very imprecise. Don't push or throw the rifle in between targets.

Tips:

Look "through" the vision barriers if possible. The key concept of this drill is to have you moving around as you are looking for A zones while vision barriers get in the way. If you are noticing that your hits are sporadic, this is usually the problem.

Be aware of the physical position of the vision barrier while you are shooting. Make sure you stay back far enough to move through the drill without hitting your rifle on the vision barriers.

It is common that bullets skim the vision barriers on this drill. You need to be comfortable moving quickly through shooting scenarios similar to this exercise without shooting the walls or barriers.

Dryfire Workup:

Walk through the exercise very carefully. Make sure that you hold out your arms and practice tracking the A zone in three-dimensional space.

You can construct a vision barrier for your home dryfire area by simply using a range-sized target stand and a real no-shoot target. This allows you to work on the tracking component in a home setting.

Adding a black paster over the perforated letter "A" on the lower A zone is very helpful if you have issues dragging hits across the targets or finding the center of the targets. Use the pasters as a form of training wheels in live-fire and dryfire to give you a specific and small spot to look at.

Go Stop

This is far from just running laps or hiking with your rifle. This drill forces you to run as hard as you can while starting and stopping in an appropriate stance allowing for immediate shooting. This drill will be exhausting after just a few reps, so work on a second drill or take time to rest before doing too many repetitions back to back.

Procedure:

Start at cone 1 in the hunt position with the safety on. Upon the start signal, engage the target associated with cone 1, then move to cone 2 and engage the appropriate target. After cone 2, move back to cone 1 and engage the associated target. Continue systematically working through the cones in this order, finishing after returning to cone 1 for a total of 10 rounds fired. The engagement order will be: 1 2 1 3 1

Assessment:

Acceptable: 14 seconds or less, all As and Cs
Good: 12 seconds or less, all As and Cs
Possible: under 10 seconds, all As

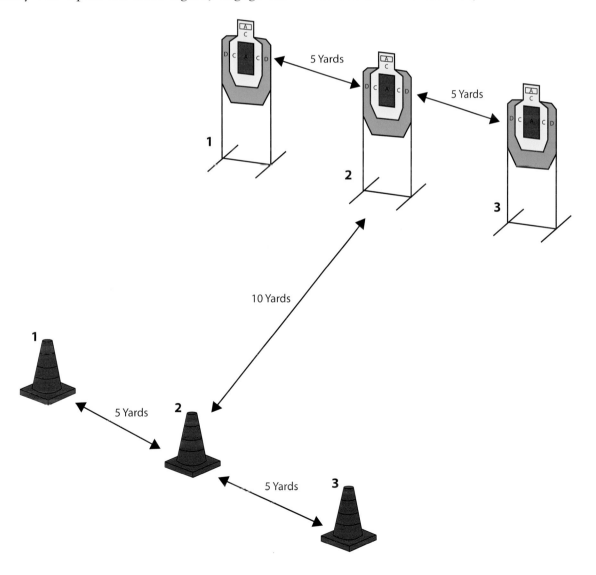

Corrections:

If you feel like you are stopping rough into a shooting position, you want to take short, small steps as you approach the next position to help you decelerate. If you attempt to stop in the space of a single step, you will likely be unable to control your body and either overrun or skid past your shooting position. You will lose time trying to restabilize yourself. Think of a baseball player running to second or third base: aggressive steps to get there, and taking smaller, shorter steps to decelerate and stop at the bag to avoid overrunning it. It is a very similar concept.

If you have widely scattered hits on the target you are engaging, make sure that you are waiting to get an appropriate sight picture on the targets after establishing a solid connection to the rifle. If you are attempting predictive shooting but your mount is not what it needs to be, the hits will become very inconsistent.

Tips:

This drill was developed by Hwansik Kim to ingrain the ability to stay low and ready to move. You should be assessing your stance every time you stop to make sure you are in a wide stance and ready to move.

Move aggressively. This drill is physically demanding; we call it a smoker. It is important that you leverage all of your athletic ability to the greatest extent possible. This drill will not be an effective training tool without going at it aggressively to produce the errors you are attempting to fix.

Do your best to get your stance set up nice and wide. You want to have the ability to efficiently move to the next shooting position when you finish shooting.

Make sure you do not have extraneous steps or movement when you exit a shooting position. This means taking small steps to change your stance. Coiling your body up like a spring or drop stepping should not occur when you are trying to move. You should stop and stabilize in a position already "preloaded" with your feet spread apart, ready to move.

Set up different variations for this drill for cone placement and target presentation. Setting up the cones in a "W"-type shape and using partial targets or steel at different distances can teach you a lot.

Dryfire Workup:

Do the drill dry. Focus on vision to cones and vision to target. That means look to where you want to go, hustle to get there, then look to a spot on the target and engage.

Positionator

This drill is very difficult. It tests your ability to get in and out of positions as well as your ability to mount the rifle from various shooting positions.

Procedure:

Start in the hunt position with the safety on. Engage the 20-yard target while standing, then engage the 30-yard target while kneeling, then go prone and shoot the 40-yard target, go back to kneeling and shoot the 30-yard target again, then stand and shoot the 20-yard target for a total of 10 rounds fired.

The 20- and 30-yard targets should have four hits per target and the 40-yard target should have two hits per target.

Assessment:

Acceptable: under 12 seconds, all As and Cs
Good: under 10 seconds, all As and Cs
Possible: under 9.0 seconds, all As and Cs (maximum of 2 Cs)

Corrections:

If you experience sporadic hits, take a close look at the aiming scheme you were using for that target.

Tips:

Keep your lead foot stable while you drop to kneeling. You don't need to move it, so hold it still. Maintain your connection to the rifle as

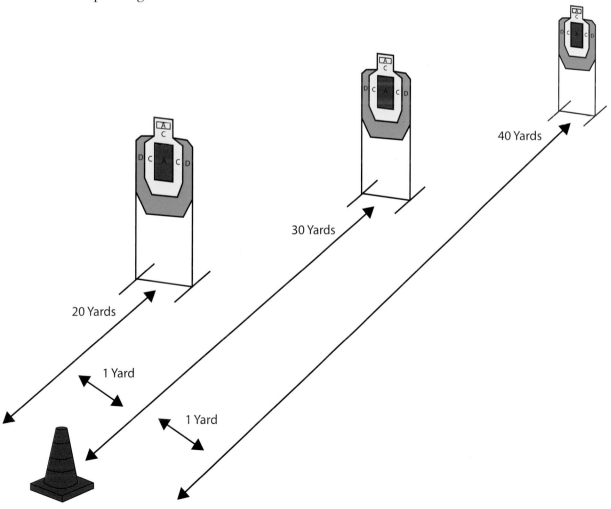

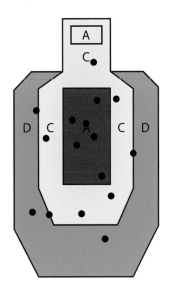

braced positions. Your rifle goes first, and you get in behind it as you change position.

Dryfire Workup:

Do the drill in dryfire. It can be set up with miniature targets on the wall. Make sure to place them in a descending pattern so your posture while prone and kneeling are realistic to what targets at real-world distances will look like. Pushing the par time down under eight seconds is very achievable in dryfire.

Variations:

Try shooting Positionator on a single target at 50 yards. All shots are taken from the standing, kneeling, and prone as previously stipulated. Try for under 15 seconds with no Deltas.

you crouch down. Be patient and shoot when you are ready on the target.

When you go prone, get your rifle to the ground first. This same thinking applies to all

GUN HANDLING

Gun handling is a test of fighting tension just as much as it is a test of technical ability. It's very easy to have your shoulders or entire upper body tense up while trying to do a fast draw or reload. The key to genuinely fast speed will be staying relaxed.

Another issue shooters encounter is when they shift their focus to the reload. Shooters often get too focused on the shooting part; they forget about the reload or they shift their focus to the reload while they should be thinking about the shooting. It's very difficult to stay relaxed while shifting your attention from task to task at the correct time.

It's very unlikely that you will get remarkably better on any of these drills while you are at the range. The biggest improvement will come from your dryfire training. While you are at the range, we suggest doing enough runs that you can draw conclusions to take back to your dryfire training, then move on to something else.

The drills included in this section are very good tests of your gun handling. You need to be able to reload your rifle in under 2.5 seconds, shot to shot, on a 10-yard target. You will need to be comfortable shouldering your rifle and engaging a target in under a second. These drills must be mastered dry and tested live or you will pay a price on all other drills.

Four Aces

This drill forces fast gun handling without allowing the shooter to sacrifice accuracy. The tight time limit will likely induce unwanted tension. Make sure you keep your shoulders relaxed as you push for speed.

Assessment:

Acceptable: 4.0 seconds, all As

Good: 3.0 seconds, all As

Possible: 2.5 seconds, all As

Corrections:

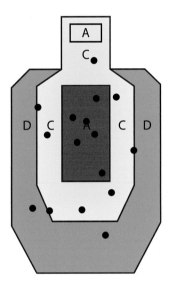

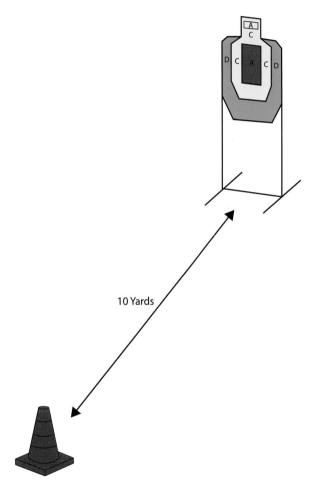

10 Yards

Inconsistent hits are likely due to an inconsistent mount of the rifle or not being specific enough with your acceptable sight picture. The rifle needs to behave the same way every time you bring it up to the target and apply pressure to control the recoil. As you increase speed, this will become difficult to do consistently.

Procedure:

Start in the hunt position with the safety on. Upon the start signal, fire two rounds into the target, reload, then fire two more rounds into the target.

Tips:

Keeping the rifle firmly connected to your shoulder while reloading will produce the fastest times for most people. If you aren't strong enough to hold the rifle in place during the reload, switch to an underarm assault reload.

If you are having issues seating the magazine on the reload, pay careful attention to the direction you are applying pressure. Make sure you are pushing the magazine straight into the rifle and not at an angle. It is useful to practice this drill both from bolt lock as well as from a closed bolt. Be sure to train both.

Dryfire Workup:

The key part of this drill is the dryfire component. We recommend working on the reloads in as simple a fashion as possible.

Start with the rifle mounted and pointed at a target. At the tone, hit the magazine release with your trigger finger and bring the fresh magazine up to the magwell. You do not insert it; just confirm it is correctly positioned. This drill can be repped quickly. Work down to a 0.80 par time or lower.

Rock Star Skills Test

This drill (designed by Erik Lund) tests gun handling, chaining multiple tasks, and your ability to stay relaxed. Due to the amount of ammo you can consume, we recommend practicing this drill in dryfire until you are comfortable with the manipulations and are ready to put your skills to the test.

Note: There are several different variations of this drill. We chose the ones we liked the best.

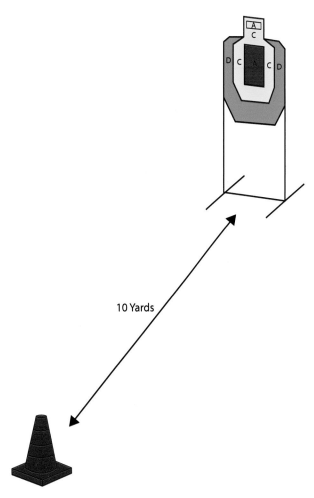

10 Yards

Procedure:

Rifle loaded with six rounds with a second six-round magazine on your belt or in a pouch. Handgun is loaded to capacity.

Start in the hunt position with the safety on. Upon the start signal, shoot the target six times with your rifle, perform a bolt lock rifle reload and shoot the target six more times, transition from an empty rifle to your pistol and shoot the target six times.

Assessment:

Acceptable: 10 seconds, all As
Good: 9.0 seconds, all As
Possible: 8.0 seconds, all As Edge of insanity: 7.5 seconds, all rifle shots into the lower A zone and all handgun shots into the upper A zone.

Corrections:

Make sure you understand to change to pistol grip technique from your rifle. It is easy to take the pistol shots for granted if you are accustomed to shooting a rifle, so be careful with the pistol shooting.

The other obvious place to get hung up here is the reload. Just make sure you set your rifle up to bolt lock and reload to a magazine with only six rounds. This will give you a safe way to practice the drill on the range.

Tips:

Force yourself to stay relaxed and try to avoid tension. Work on specific gun handling issues in isolation. You likely won't get a lot better on the drill in a single day. Doing a few reps should give you enough information to take back to your dryfire training.

Make sure you reestablish a solid connection to the rifle after the reload. When the shooting is close and fast, it is easy to lose control of your connection.

Dryfire Workup:

This drill can be run in dryfire quite easily. Start with an empty magazine in your rifle and your rifle at bolt lock. Reload to a magazine of dummy rounds and then transition to your pistol. A very good par time for dryfire on this drill is six seconds.

80 to 10

This drill is a good test of your ability to shoot accurately and manipulate your gun under stress.

Procedure:

Start with a pair of rifle magazines loaded with three rounds each and a full handgun.

The drill is Virginia count, meaning extra shots are not allowed. Completing the drill with all C zone (or better) hits in under 35 seconds is a good basic standard of proficiency. This drill can also be shot on a C zone steel plate in place of a paper USPSA target.

80 yards: two rounds rifle
60 yards: two rounds rifle (one, reload, one)
40 yards: two rounds rifle
20 yards: two rounds pistol
10 yards: two rounds pistol

Assessment:

Acceptable: 35 seconds or less, all As and Cs
Good: 30 seconds or less, all As and Cs
Possible: 25 seconds or less, all As and Cs

Corrections:

The most common problem at distance is getting proper sight alignment on the target. Because you are firing two shots per yard line,

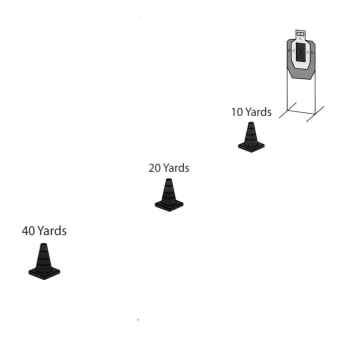

10 Yards

20 Yards

40 Yards

60 Yards

80 Yards

you need to take a follow-up shot. This means it can be very difficult to recover the sights to the correct aimpoint without focusing on the sights themselves. This requires constant attention on this drill. We do recommend turning your dot down when you get back past 50 yards.

When you are shooting closer to the target, be patient. You need to avoid rushing even though you are getting closer and closer to the target. Rushing is an easy way to fail this exercise.

Tips:

This drill tests your patience, especially as you start making an effort to shoot it more and more aggressively. There is no room for mistakes when it comes to your accuracy, so you need to be very patient and allow the sights to line up and press the trigger carefully from each yard line. This sounds simple, but the amount of running involved in this drill means you need to really settle down into position before you shoot. Your heart will be pounding by the end of the drill. Patience is really the biggest struggle here.

Some shooters will have no issue making the shots, but they will struggle to bring the aggression level to the rest of the exercise. Achieving a good score on this drill involves running and gun handling at top speed while shooting at a controlled pace. It is difficult to "change gears." Mental rehearsals can help you maximize aggression on the non-shooting parts of the drill if you have an issue with that.

When you are running forward with your rifle slung, keep your support hand on the rifle in order to stabilize it. This will make the running much easier. Placing your support hand on the stock once the rifle is slung is probably the best way to do it, but feel free to experiment.

Dryfire workup:

One thing to practice dry is running with a slung rifle. The movement on this drill from the 40- to the 20-yard line will be with the rifle slung and it can be a little bit strange if you don't practice it. Make sure that you stabilize your rifle with your support arm and keep your pistol ready to go in your firing hand.

STANDARDS

When you are training, it is very important to have specific goals to meet. The standard tests in this book should give you some clear goals and give you something to grow into.

CQB Warmup is the assessment that this book is built on. It tests you in many different ways and is a complicated multi-string event. CQB Warmup is a really good test for just this reason. You need to carry out a fair bit of shooting and do things correctly throughout or you won't pass. It is a very adaptable test that scales well as you improve. Scoring it using hit factor is a very good test for advanced shooters.

El Presidente ("El Prez") is a classic test of shooting ability. Try this drill along with some of the variations. Consistently shooting El Prez in under six seconds is pretty good. It's very possible to shoot it in under five seconds.

Below is a chart of some goal times for a wide variety of skill tests. These aren't the fastest possible times, but they will serve as a good guideline to assess your performance.

	10 yards	15 yards	25 yards	50 yards
Ready Up Two Shots from Hunt Position	0.8	1	1.2	1.5
Mag Change from Bolt Lock to Alpha	1.7	2	2.2	3
Doubles Drill Split Goal	max	max	0.25	0.4
4 Aces	3	3.5	4	6
Bill Drill	1.5	1.8	2	3.5
El Prez Drill	6	7	8	10
Blake Drill	2	2.5	3	4
Rifle Cross Drill	4.5 (3 C max)	X	X	X

El Presidente

This drill will test your ability to combine target transitions, fast aggressive shooting, and gun handling. It sets a very reasonable standard for you to be able to string these skills together.

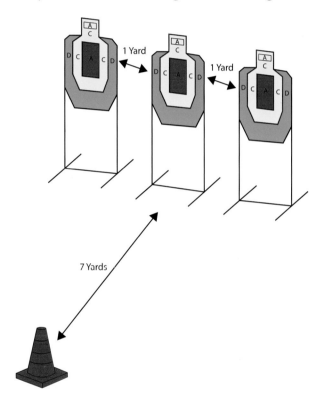

Procedure:

Start facing up range in the hunt position with the rifle on safe. Upon the start signal, turn and engage each target with two rounds each, reload, then shoot each target with two rounds again. Your rifle should be set up to go to bolt lock before the reload (loaded with five rounds in the magazine and one in the chamber).

Assessment:

Acceptable: 7.5 seconds, no Ds
Good: under 6.0 seconds, no Ds
Possible: under 5.0 seconds, no Ds

Corrections:

If the first target you are shooting has a much larger pattern than the others, make sure you are being critical of your vision while turning your head. Your eyes should snap to the center of the target, then maintain the visual patience to see the dot on the target before you start shooting.

Be sure you nail the mount of your rifle. If you don't get the rifle in the correct position, it will not behave properly for you.

Tips:

Make sure that you get a solid connection to your rifle. This applies to the turn and the reload. It is important for your recoil control to get that solid connection, but it is hard to do on this drill because of how busy the gun handling is. If you aren't using a muzzle brake or a suppressor, this drill will feel much more challenging.

Dryfire Workup:

This drill is a popular and effective dryfire training tool, in addition to being a good live-fire assessment. It is strongly recommended that you work on El Prez in dryfire. Set your rifle to bolt lock, then load a magazine of dummy rounds. In this fashion you can quickly and effectively complete training repetitions and practice realistically releasing the bolt.

If your dryfire is realistic in terms of assessment, the times will be similar to your times with live ammo. With live ammo, missing your mount will punish you by making the rifle harder to control. This will not show up in dryfire unless you are honest with yourself.

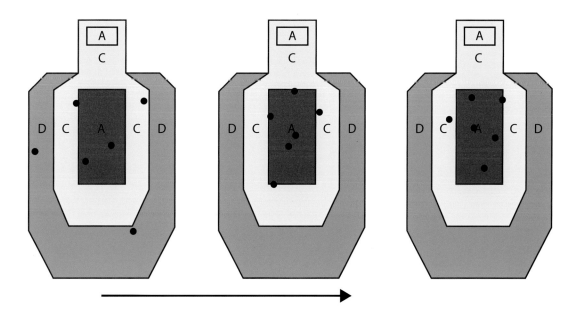

The other thing to pay attention to during dryfire is the turn and mount you need to do for the first target on El Prez. Make sure you snap your head to the target first to give you a visual target to bring your red dot to. Make sure you focus on establishing a firm connection to the rifle and your shoulder. This is the connection you would need to get good control with live ammo.

Variations:

If you are unable to do the traditional up-range start for El Prez due to range restrictions or other safety concerns, feel free to start facing the targets. This should subtract about a half a second from your total time. Consider this with respect to the assessments laid out above.

If you would like to start with the rifle and then transition to pistol, that makes for an excellent variation on El Prez. Set your rifle up to go empty after six rounds so you can safely transition to pistol and fire the next six rounds. This variation should take roughly the same time as the rifle variation. It may be a bit faster especially if you aren't using a retention holster.

Consider shooting El Prez at 50 yards. Under 10 seconds with all A or C zone hits (no Ds) is considered quite good shooting in some circles. Shooting that score requires you to do everything right. You need a good turn and index on the targets, a good reload and a really good mount. If you don't hit your mount, your rifle will not return properly and the drill will probably not turn out well. If you are quick at 10 yards, try working your way back to 50 yards and you will learn a lot.

CQB Warmup

This is the final test. This combines all the skills you have been training on.

This is a complicated and difficult test. Matt Pranka uses this exercise in his classes for law enforcement officers. As of this writing, only a tiny group of people have passed this in one of his classes. It is a good test of multiple elements of your shooting.

The drill involves multiple strings of fire requiring 48 rounds of ammunition. There are 36 rounds required with your rifle and 12 from your pistol. You will need to sling your rifle and transition to your holstered pistol. You will also need to perform an emergency reload of your rifle from bolt lock.

You begin at 40 yards and shoot at a very aggressive pace with the rifle. You then shoot from 40 yards and advance to 20 yards. Then you go from 20 yards to 10 yards. Then you start working gun handling, including both pistol and rifle shooting from 10 yards and 7 yards. It is a very well-rounded test of your abilities.

We recommend one or two attempts of the drill at a time. Study the results and locate the area or areas in which you are lacking and then train drills appropriate for those deficiencies.

This drill is calibrated for duty-style equipment. The rifles used in its design had no compensators or suppressors. They had two-stage triggers. The holsters had at least level II retention. The rifles had red dot sights without magnification. The pistols were 9mm Glocks. Consider this when assessing your score and compare this equipment to what you are using. Using a rifle with iron sights would make this much harder. Using an aggressive muzzle brake would make the 40-yard shooting much easier.

The strings of fire are structured to have built-in safety measures. The intention is that you start with a 30-round magazine and never fire extra shots. In this way you transition from the rifle to pistol only when the rifle is empty (after firing 30 rounds). Make sure when you are running with the rifle you apply the safety. Remember, you shouldn't be in a hurry to reholster your pistol. By following these rules, you should minimize the chance of an accidental discharge.

We have four standards for CQB Warmup. The normal standard is the one we think you should train to. It requires you to be able to apply predictive shooting at the 40-yard line. If you can't do this, you will not meet the par time. You will also be required to have fast and confident gun handling - transitions, reloads and movement are all tested.

For intermediate-level shooters, the Relaxed Standard should apply. Getting the shots off in time at the 40-yard line is a killer for many shooters, especially when they are new to this style of rifle shooting and their equipment doesn't have an aggressive recoil control device. In this standard, you just add one second to each of the 40-yard strings. Because of this, the Relaxed Standard gives the shooter that can't shoot fast at 40 yards a better chance to shoot a passing score.

For new shooters, we recommend the Basic Standard. You shoot the same course of fire at a reactive shooting pace. This allows you to build

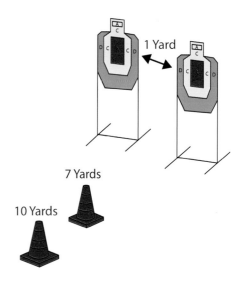

1 Yard

7 Yards

10 Yards

20 Yards

40 Yards

accuracy and consistency until you are prepared to attack the standards at a more aggressive pace.

Hit factor scoring is another way to try CQB Warmup after you have a good grasp of the exercise. Every one hundredth of a second counts in hit factor scoring, so it can really help polish your shooting.

Range setup: Two scorable targets (USPSA/IPSC) per shooter. Firing lines distinguishable at 7 yards, 10 yards, 20 yards, and 40 yards.

Start position for each string is the hunt position (rifle stock shouldered, sights below your eye line with the safety on) unless otherwise stipulated.

From the 40-yard line: Upon the start signal, fire two rounds per target from a standing position, then transition to a prone position and fire two more rounds per target (eight rounds total). Par time: 6.0 seconds.

From the 40-yard line, ending at the 20-yard line: Upon the start signal, fire two rounds per target from a standing position, then move up to the 20-yard line and fire two more rounds per target from a standing position (eight rounds total). Par time: 9.0 seconds.

From the 20-yard line, ending at the 10-yard line: Upon the start signal, fire two rounds per target from a standing position, then move up to the 10-yard line and fire two more rounds per target from a standing position (eighty rounds total). Par time: 7.0 seconds.

From the 10-yard line: Upon the start signal, fire three rounds per target, transition to pistol and fire three rounds per target (six rounds rifle and six rounds pistol total). Par time: 6.0 seconds.

From the 7-yard line, start with an empty rifle, shouldered, mag inserted, bolt locked open, weapon on fire, aiming at target through sights: Upon the start signal, transition to pistol and fire three rounds per target (six rounds pistol total). Par time: 3.0 seconds.

From the 7-yard line, start with an empty rifle, shouldered, mag inserted, bolt locked open, weapon on fire, aiming at target through sights: Upon the start signal, reload the rifle and engage each target with three rounds (six rounds total). Par time: 5.0 seconds.

Scoring: Each target has 18 rifle and six pistol hits required.

Total possible points are 240. Each round fired has a maximum of five points. USPSA/IPSC target is the standard: A = 5 points, B/C = 3 points, D = 1 point, Miss = 0 points. Add total points scored.

Any rounds fired more than 0.30 seconds after the par time are considered overtime shots. Overtime shots are considered misses and carry an additional five-point penalty (remove five points from your final score for each overtime shot).

A passing score is 85 percent (204 points) or better. Shooting above 230 is very impressive.

Shooting a perfect score has been done by few. Consider running this test with duty equipment.

Tips:

Challenge yourself to learn to consistently shoot a passing score on this test. It's a good benchmark for your skills. Perfect scores are possible if you can nail the standing 40-yard shooting just right.

Don't rush your shooting, especially once you move forward of the 40-yard line. The times allow you to shoot at a controlled pace provided you are snappy with your movement and manipulations. Do not throw points away because you were rushing. This exercise is scored purely on points, assuming you make the time limit. Do not rush.

The 40-yard standing shooting is the most difficult part of the test. The time limits will require you to shoot predictively, so you need to have a consistent mount. This is really the easiest place to drop points.

If you have weaknesses in your dryfire, they will be exposed by the second half of CQB Warmup. Make sure you can index your rifle, transition to pistol, and reload your rifle properly. The time limits are such that you will need to rush the shooting if you fumble your manipulations, and that could lead to lost points. You don't need to be super quick, but you need to be precise.

CQB Warmup Relaxed Standard

This "relaxed" standard is a fair test for someone that hasn't mastered predictive shooting with their rifle yet. The 40-yard strings with the rifle have one second added to each, allowing you to shoot reacting to each sight picture.

Range setup: Two scorable targets (USPSA/IPSC) per shooter. Firing lines distinguishable at 7 yards, 10 yards, 20 yards, and 40 yards.

Start position for each string is the hunt position (rifle stock shouldered, sights below your eye line with the safety on) unless otherwise stipulated.

From the 40-yard line: Upon the start signal, fire two rounds per target from a standing position, then transition to a prone position and fire two more rounds per target (eight rounds total). Par time: 7.0 seconds.

From the 40-yard line, ending at the 20-yard line: Upon the start signal, fire two rounds per target from a standing position, then move up to the 20-yard line and fire two more rounds per target from a standing position (eight rounds total). Par time: 10 seconds.

From the 20-yard line, ending at the 10-yard line: Upon the start signal, fire two rounds per target from a standing position, then move up to the 10-yard line and fire two more rounds per target from a standing position (eight rounds total). Par time: 7.0 seconds.

From the 10-yard line: Upon the start signal, fire three rounds per target, transition to pistol and fire three rounds per target (six rounds rifle and six rounds pistol total). Par time: 6.0 seconds.

From the 7 yard line, start with an empty rifle, shouldered, mag inserted, bolt locked open, weapon on fire, aiming at target through sights: Upon the start signal, transition to pistol and fire three rounds per target (six rounds pistol total). Par time: 3.0 seconds.

From the 7-yard line, start with an empty rifle, shouldered, mag inserted, bolt locked open, weapon on fire, aiming at target through sights: Upon the start signal, reload the rifle and engage each target with three rounds (six rounds total). Par time: 5.0 seconds.

Scoring: Each target has 18 rifle and six pistol hits required.

Total possible points are 240. Each round fired has a maximum of five points. USPSA/IPSC target is the standard: A = 5 points, B/C = 3 points, D = 1 point, Miss = 0 points. Add total points scored.

Any rounds fired more than 0.30 seconds after the par time are considered overtime shots. Overtime shots are considered misses and carry an additional five-point penalty (remove five points from your final score for each overtime shot).

A passing score is 85 percent (204 points) or better.

After passing this standard, please attack the proper CQB Warmup standard.

CQB Warmup Basic Standard

The Basic Standard is a fair test for someone that hasn't mastered the previous drills in this book. Shoot CQB Warmup and note your times. Shoot the drill at a reactive pace.

Pay attention to your sights and shoot when they return. Track your time and note your total time for the entire drill. Simply add each string together.

The total time goal for CQB Warmup Basic Standard is 40 seconds. When your total time is under 40 seconds and your points are above 220, attack a faster standard on this drill.

Range setup: Two scorable targets (USPSA/IPSC) per shooter. Firing lines distinguishable at 7 yards, 10 yards, 20 yards, and 40 yards.

Start position for each string is the hunt position (rifle stock shouldered, sights below your eye line with the safety on) unless otherwise stipulated.

From the 40-yard line: Upon the start signal, fire two rounds per target from a standing position, then transition to a prone position and fire two more rounds per target (eight rounds total).

From the 40-yard line, ending at the 20-yard line: Upon the start signal, fire two rounds per target from a standing position, then move up to the 20-yard line and fire two more rounds per target from a standing position (eight rounds total).

From the 20-yard line, ending at the 10-yard line: Upon the start signal, fire two rounds per target from a standing position, then move up to the 10-yard line and fire two more rounds per target from a standing position (eight rounds total).

From the 10-yard line: Upon the start signal, fire three rounds per target, transition to pistol and fire three rounds per target (six rounds rifle and six rounds pistol total).

From the 7-yard line, start with an empty rifle, shouldered, mag inserted, bolt locked open, weapon on fire, aiming at target through sights: Upon the start signal, transition to pistol and fire three rounds per target (six rounds pistol total).

From the 7-yard line, start with an empty rifle, shouldered, mag inserted, bolt locked open, weapon on fire, aiming at target through sights: Upon the start signal, reload the rifle and engage each target with three rounds (six rounds total).

Scoring: Each target has 18 rifle and six pistol hits required.

Total possible points are 240. Each round fired has a maximum of five points. USPSA/IPSC target is the standard: A = 5 points, B/C = 3 points, D = 1 point, Miss = 0 points. Add total points scored.

A passing score is 85 percent (204 points) or better.

CQB Warmup Hit Factor Standard

An alternative way to score CQB Warmup is to use hit factor scoring. This means scoring the exercise with total points divided by total time. The minimum score of 204 points done in the maximum allowable time (36 seconds assuming all the time is used) is 5.6666, for example.

By tracking the total time for each string of fire and adding it up, you are accounting for the actual time used. If you compare this method of scoring to the standard test, you are rewarded by shooting faster. You can achieve a higher score if you shoot that way, but you risk points being dropped if you shoot with less accuracy. It is a very challenging system.

Shooting this drill above a hit factor of 7.0 is very difficult. This will require you to undercut the standard drill string times by a few seconds and still maintain an easily passing score. If you can undercut the string times in the standard drill by five or six seconds and you only drop a few Charlies, you will get above a 7.5 hit factor. That's a very good score, especially with duty-style rifles not equipped with recoil-reducing muzzle devices. Scoring above an 8.0 hit factor is pretty insane shooting.

OTHER TITLES WITH SKYHORSE PUBLISHING

Breakthrough Marksmanship
Ben Stoeger
120 Pages
ISBN: 978-1-5107-7936-5
Price: $15.99

Practical Pistol
Ben Stoeger
216 Pages
ISBN: 978-1-5107-7948-8
Price: $24.99

Practical Shooting Training
Ben Stoeger, Joel Park
336 Pages
ISBN: 978-1-5107-7934-1
Price: $29.99

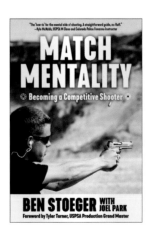

Match Mentality
Ben Stoeger, Joel Park
304 Pages
ISBN: 978-1-5107-7941-9
Price: $24.99